how to talk at gin

how
to talk
at gin

ERNIE
KOVACS

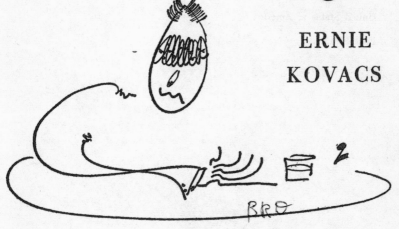

ILLUSTRATED BY THE AUTHOR IN A
MOMENT OF OVERCONFIDENCE

1962 garden city, n.y.
doubleday & company, inc.

Library of Congress

Catalog Card Number 62–9325

Copyright © 1962 by Doubleday & Company, Inc.,

Trustee of the Estate of Ernie Kovacs

Printed in the

United States of America

First Edition

DEDICATION

This book is dedicated to that wonderful little restaurant (whose name escapes me at the moment) in Verona, Italy, or perhaps it was in the Poconos in Pennsylvania, where they served that superb Wiener Schnitzel or roast pork or whatever it was.

SERIOUSLY DEDICATED TO MY MOTHER

BIBLIOGRAPHY

How to Make Instant Pâté de Foie Gras

Water Fountains at Home and a Broad

How to Grease a Tuba

Recommended Summer Camps and Shady Motels

Low Calorie Lard

Newark, New Jersey

Varicose Veins Can Be Fun

Wetbacks in Old Mexico and Dry Martinis in Manhattan

Does the DC-7 Eat Its Young?

Crockery Isn't All It's Cracked Up to Be

I Was a Hungarian Chess and Checkers Champion

How to Mount a Large, Gray Squirrel

I Was a Chukker in Polo, New Hampshire

One More Time, Lucy Monroe!

Esso's Map of Hightstown, New Jersey

There's More to John Philip Sousa Than Meets the Eye

Nuclear Fission at Home

Ice Hockey . . . by Dame May Whitty

PREFACE

*(A DEVICE USED TO SUCKER PEOPLE
INTO BUYING BOOKS.)*

A BADLY TORN 2 OF SPADES

Within these pages, there is nothing whatsoever to be learned about the playing of gin rummy.

There are already dozens of books on the open market which explain the subtleties of the game. Some of the books tell you how to play gin and some tell you how to detect cheaters. The authors illustrate this by exposing their methods. Actually, this latter type is simply a sly way of selling books which tell you HOW to cheat. And, because cheating is fun and lucrative, many of these books sell quite well. It is interesting to note that while the authors of both groups are in complete disagreement on how to play or how to cheat properly, they all agree that ten cards are dealt to each player.[1] This number is always constant. (Give or take a few in the case of a nervous dealer.)

Gin rummy has provided employment for many people in the manufacture of accessories. WE–THEY has been printed more times than "These matches were stolen from the Garfinkles." It[2] has been more respon-

A 2 OF SPADES NOT AS BADLY TORN

sible for marital bickering than loose red hairs on seersucker lapels.

The game is played for money on occasion with the amount per point varying from 1/10 cent to $10. (The players in the $10 group are somewhat prone to prognostication in the matter of liquidating the resultant obligations.)

Gin is as time consuming as an ostrich eating pocket watches. The serious gin player's body is occupied

[1] Bear this in mind.

[2] Gin.

Note: Footnote #1 even if not so labeled could be so assumed that because it is not numbered Footnote #2, it must therefore be Footnote #1.

more with gin than with the natural processes of elimination. (Of which there are three.)

It is played all over the world. (In Arabia, it is called Djnn . . . or something very similar to that.) It is played a great deal in Hollywood, where a case on record recalls a tyrannical studio head who used to have the cleaning women bring him any wastebaskets in which they found gin scores. There was a code number on the bottom of each basket and simply by consulting his decoder, he knew whom to fire. After a bit, the employee whose wastebasket was not returned accepted this as a sign of automatic dismissal, much the same as a mahout not being assigned a loin cloth for a big parade in India.

Gin is played on land, sea, in planes, and in places not suitable for public discussion. In planes, the game begins so fast, the sound of the riffle of the deck is often confused with the clicking of the safety belt being uncoupled.

However, in the many volumes written about gin, no writer has discussed the *dialogue and attitudes* to be used when playing. The use of the well-turned cliché is the mark of the pro.

This book, then, will attempt to supply such information, and by assiduously assimilating the facts herein, the reader in then applying himself will be able to prove that the *best* gin player is by no means the *greatest* gin player. This is a book being written with considerable reflection, much love, and not a little pain. True, there is a quiescent purpose of financial gain in mind but the missionary zeal of the author is his main effort.[3]

[3] Avoid dull needles and use a soft cloth.

HOW THE TITLE WAS SELECTED

"Well, what shall we call our book, John?" I said, chuckling. John is our stripling of a maid . . . she was so-named because of her deep voice and her affinity for stripling at a moment's notice.

"I don' know, Marse Tom," she replied, using a Butterfly McQueen image, "I jess don' know." And she leaned over and gave me a big, fat kiss. Being nobody's fool, she quickly realized her petite indiscretion and to cover it went around the room giving everyone a kiss including each of the many pets about the house. Unfortunately, we have a bowl full of guppies and by the time she kissed them all, she had drowned. But we love her still. In fact, I was going to name the book after her (*JOHN*) but what with the intimacy she had displayed on her final night, together with the fact that she still lay near the guppy bowl with a plastic mouth-to-mouth respirator tube in the same position as when we had last communicated, I felt it might cause talk and began throwing myself about wildly for other titles.

Because the reading and television public is somewhat prone to favoring more serious fare, my working title was: *The Rise and Demise of Gothic Type*. When this was presented to the publisher, his eyelids lowered seductively and he made gestures such as described in best-sellers. Tearing the manuscript from his perspiring hands and resisting his advances with neat parries and some thrusts (for I have other means of support and do not have to subject myself to this kind of thing simply to make an extra buck), I said, "Ho-ho, I see we shall have to try a less exciting title if we are to make use of Uncle Sam's many mail rooms."

A neighbor, whose philosophy is at its peak when he is saying things like "beating plowshares into swords" and other somewhat similarly esoteric phrases, suggested the title imply some racy things about public figures. Most of these were rather one-tracked and the basic thought was to infer embezzlement of past presidents and indiscretions of international philanthropists. Weighing the time involved in getting clearances from the heirs against the doubtful value of the implications, I contemplated, instead, something current at the time of the writing of this material. One thought was to give the impression that this book contained a complete list of the various American airplanes being hijacked by Cuba. *Fidel Castro, Philatelist* was the title . . . (many of the planes were *stamped* with the company's name) . . . but the list was under constant change and when President Kennedy got tough, I felt that it would be illogical to present such a thick book for such a thin list.

The Art of Jewish Cooking, Where to Dine in Passaic, New Jersey, Appendectomies at Home, and *Puberty Can Be Fun* were all discarded for various reasons of whimsy. And so I hit upon the present title. (Actually, as I write this, I have no title at all but a preface of this kind can hardly be ended on *that* note.)

HOLLOW GRATITUDE SECTION

Besides the works mentioned in the bibliography, I would like also to express my more-or-less abject thanks to the following who made this book possible:

The Bicycle and Bee playing card manufacturers.

The Eberhard Faber pencil company. (Hb division, also soft.)

The Jack Daniels, Chivas Regal, and Beefeater folks, my constant companions through the many candlelit hours dedicated to this work.

My desk.

My three children (Betty, Kippie, and Mia) without whose (wonderful) interruptions this book would have been finished three months earlier and therefore much before its time.

Joe Mikalos, a friend who, after playing only twice with me, told me I had no business playing the game.

To all those who have won money from me at gin and therefore made it necessary for me to write this in order to get some of it back. (Those who *lost* to me I sneer at as being pretty darned stupid.)

The magnificent giant redwoods of California from whose pulp comes the paper that makes gin rummy score pads. (Please do not write and tell me that I am misinformed on this as I feel redwood trees are romantic and I really do not give a damn in the first place.)

Kim Novak, who only plays for 1/4 a cent a point, but she has so many other things going for her that somehow I have never really cared about the money.

Irving Arab, who invented Arabic numerals for keeping score.

Enrico Caruso.

chapter one

THE HOST

LET'S GET THOSE BOYS OUT OF
THE TRENCHES AND HOME BY CHRISTMAS!

Hosting a gin game is exacting yet rewarding, much as raising raccoons for fun and profit. It is the host who is expected to set the intellectual level of the imminent *parry* and *thrust* of the evening.[1]

It differs from bridge and canasta mainly in the initial setting up of the table and other equipment. When friends come over for an evening of bridge, it is customary to see the card table, pads, cards, pencils, etc., already in place with little ash trays and cocktail coasters with humorous sayings already in place. *Not so with gin rummy!*

Most people who play gin do so to excess. This finally results in a shyness within them and they are reluctant to admit, even among themselves, that their

[1] Italics are used here as "parry" derives from the Italian *"parare"* meaning that the possible legitimacy of the male *parent* is doubtful. Italians are great gin players. Even of disposition, slow to excitement . . . all this makes a good gin player. (See footnote to footnote.)

17

only communicable relationship (see footnote just following footnote labeled "F to F") is the constant pursuit of the game. The greenest novitiate to the game knows better than to have his players arrive to see a white gin rummy pad and blue and red pencils lying in good composition. Regardless of the fact that these men have summoned each other that evening for the express playing of gin, the actual beginning of play must appear as an *improvisation of the moment*. (Even in the earlier discussions over the phone, gin is only mentioned as an afterthought: *Viz*: "Why don't you and the boys come over this evening. We'll kind of sit and stare at each other. May play some gin, huh?")

To illustrate the preliminaries of an evening of gin, let us parallel with a boy and a girl who are about to consummate the evening with that other grand game. In this worthy, albeit time-consuming, boy-girl *divertissement*, the act itself must avoid any appearances of premeditation. Any mechanical contrivances involved must appear as though by magic and only when immediately called upon. *It is quite impossible to make the irrelevant small talk of propriety when either of the participants has just ducked into some beaded vestibule to accouter himself or herself with any of the physical products of civilization.*[2]

F to F: This is also true of Hungarians.
Footnote as indicated above: The Germans picturesquely refer to this as *raison d'etre*.
[2] As this is not a medical tome nor does it appear it will be a best-seller, we cannot go into graphic detail as to just what the hell we are talking about.

In either gin or the other activity, the entire exhilaration of togetherness flies out the window when once it (either gin or the other) appears cut and dried.[3] The *feign of surprise* is half the fun.

To return to the preliminary moments of the gin game: A conversation is first entered into on what might best be described as on a generic level.[4] That is to say, questions are posed which require nothing more than ambiguous response or affirmative nod. The phrasing of each question is so that it will discourage, or at least *not encourage*, continuation of the subject. The obvious reason for this is the avoiding of long, involved discussions that might prolong the beginning of the game. Why any conversation at all, then?[5]

The answer is simply this: If the game were to begin immediately, these four members of the community would take on the appearance of degenerates whose sole purpose in convening was for the playing of cards.

Let us put to examination and illustration the type of questions and answers that have been most successful. Each is almost completion in itself and each *cleverly leads toward conclusion of discussion*.

Taking first the earlier mentioned case of the boy and girl, the *construction* of dialogue will be similar. In this case, the technical term best describing this conversation is *Dialogue à Disrobemente*.[6]

[3] An unfortunate expression in the latter case.
[4] This footnote has nothing to do with the word "generic." It simply is used to substantiate that old saying, "Three footnotes to the page and your book is all the rage."
[5] Good question. (Also, now you can ignore Footnote #3.)
[6] A bientôt!

A good opener:

"Say, isn't that a new Modigliani?"

Note that a "Yes, it is," or "No, it isn't," in response will not only answer the question and keep up the appearance of conversation but will *terminate the discussion of this subject!*

Other phrases for variation or follow-up:

"The automobile show opened in New York today."

When the actual showing of the automobile show is so far away that the question becomes palpably silly, a flick into international affairs is acceptable:

"Macmillan was quite good at the UN."[7]

It is important to note that none of these queries has ended with, "——, don't you?" "Don't you?" by the use of the personal pronoun and the raised inflection solicits more than "aye" or "nay" and requires personal viewpoint if the person to whom the question is directed is worth his salt at all.

Now the conversation is ready to proceed toward questions cleverly designed to bring things to a focal point.[8] He speaks:

"I like the way you are doing your hair."

This is *particularly good* as she, observing becoming modesty, must refrain from anything other than a throaty, "Thenk yew, John."[9]

[7] Here a broader horizon is touched upon and one can almost smell crumpets and hear the friendly click of the umbrella (or *"brolly,"* as it is sometimes called in London).

[8] If you will excuse the expression in this family publication.

[9] Or "Tom" or "Pete" or "Julius," depending upon the name of the person involved.

Also, it will be seen that a remark dedicated to any part of the body has the further advantage of potential personal examination.

"You must have been out in the sun a great deal this past weekend." The stature and the possibilities of follow-up of THAT one is staggering to the everyday mind. Another goodie:

"Say, that's an interesting mole!"[10]

What an exciting comparison to gin rummy must now be obvious to the reader! Our gin players are seated. One speaks:

"Isn't that a new Picasso?"

Another:

"They had a hell of a crowd at the automobile show."

The third:

"I - didn't - realize - Macmillan - was - so - tall - let's - play - gin."

The more succinct layout here would indicate that this group was more anxious to play gin than the boy and girl were to—[11]

[10] This is usually the last word heard in the room.
[11] On second thought, forget this footnote.

HOW TO SAY HELLO

CARMEN, GET THAT G.D. ROSE OUTTA YOUR MOUTH,
I CAN'T UNDERSTAND A WORD YOU'RE SAYING!

As Clyde Beatty knew the peculiarities of each of his performing cats and as anyone knows the implication of the hair cream advertisement "Does she or doesn't she?", so the perfect host of the gin game knows the dark winding passageways of the mind that make the greeting of each player specific and peculiar *to* that guest. The phrases, while appearing somewhat acidulous, are so *standardized* that they cannot cause offense.[12]

Here now, for examination and notation, are some of these salutary utterances:

"Here's my pigeon!"

Dynamite! Here the host has neatly executed gin rum-

[12] There are exceptions, of course, with extremely sensitive players and should the author think of it, they will be dealt with later in the book.

my's most immemorial triplet of words.[13] Despite its rather abrupt construction, this is a phrase to be handled with the delicacy of a corneal transplant. It is the *leitmotiv* of gin. In the mouth of the novice, it is as treacherous as a rabid parakeet in a bent cage.[14] See now the line, *ostensibly the same,* delivered vaguely by a *nouveau ginnast*:

"Well, here's the pigeon!"

Catastrophe! Catasthrophic and grievous! The article "THE" has appeared where the possessive pronoun "MY" once was! The inference that the pigeon's stupidity has been discussed in his absence has now dropped with the embarrassment of soiled underwear from an executive's briefcase. He has been branded with the Scarlet Letter. Referring to him as "MY pigeon" is an intimate arm-about-the-shoulder camaraderie used only when, incidentally, his losses are $1.75 or less. (If, however, even this small loss has occurred on more than two successive occasions, a simple, "Hello, Harry," is more advisable.) Let us illustrate further by returning to our boy and girl and examining a similar circumstance of dialogue:

"Your mustache tickles."

We instantly see an inflated male[15] smirking contentedly at his hirsute *fait accompli*. Now let us examine:

---

[13] "Pigeon" is derived from the Greek, *sucari*, loosely translated as "sucker."

[14] Or Mynah bird.

[15] No other implication here than a reference to ego.

"The mustache tickles."

You want more trouble than this? The use of "THE" in this instance is as dangerous as nitroglycerine bubble gum. Implications?

a—*Like the girls told me the other day at bridge, your mustache really does tickle.*

b—"All mustaches (*and there have been many in my past*) tickle."

c—She is a foreigner (or worse, a foreign spy) and has learned the English language from an instruction booklet. *Viz:* THE pencil is on THE table; THE aunt is sick; THE hat is on crooked; THE postcard is too expensive, do you have one which is THE cheaper?

HOW TO REPLY

I DIDN'T RAISE MY CLAVICLE TO BE A SHOULDER.

The individual (personalities aside for the moment) who is addressed as "my pigeon" answers in one of these Victorian pronouncements:

"What I am going to do to you tonight is going to break my heart."[16]

Or:

"You mean, you fool, you actually SENT for me?"

Or:

"Charlie, I am going to take your ass tonight."

You have been given the most basic of gin greetings. To reiterate (for it is important) any references to *pigeon* are to be avoided with a *constant loser*. This does not hold true of ALL constant losers, but as the author cannot possibly know all of each reader's friends, he must leave it at that. Dealing with the CONSTANT LOSER is a touchy thing, but handled prop-

[16] German gin players say *"mein herz."*

erly, it *can* be managed. Here is a phrase to be used in greeting the steady loser which is casual but inherently *beau geste* in construction:

"Did you manage to find parking space in the car port, Larry?"[17]

Another gay rejoinder:

"Hey, where did you get the crazy sport shirt?!"[18]

The CONSTANT WINNER may be addressed in almost any manner and with practically complete abandon as he is impossible to offend:

"Hello, killer."

Or:

"Who asked YOU to come?!"

It is, in fact, unnecessary to greet him at all.

It is a school of split decision as to whether it is wise to invite The Boss. One area of thought has it that this makes one's losses tax deductible, while another area has it that this is not so. However, if he *has* been invited, it is certainly necessary to greet him in the fashion of those who gather for cards and these phrases of *quasi-awe* and *simulated good-fellowship* are quite acceptable:

"Hey, fellows, here's the guy we've got to watch tonight!"

The comments of the others will depend on their places of employment. If they are employed by the same firm,

[17] It is a good idea to consider the inadvisability of this remark on an individual who has lost his car through constant gambling.
[18] To be used only in the instance of his *wearing* a sport shirt as the implied sincerity of the greeting is somewhat lessened if he is *not* wearing a sport shirt.

there will be hasty affirmation, if they work elsewhere they will ignore the entire conversation and go about hanging up their coats. Sometimes, there is the case of the employee whose position is in shaky stage and in his overeagerness to get the same point across sometimes strips the phrase of its frosting and a certain amount of discomfort is felt by the others present when he blurts:

"Wow, what a player!!"[19]

PLAYER WHO HAS BROUGHT GIRL TO GAME

Thus we know how to welcome THE CONSTANT WINNER, THE CONSTANT LOSER, and THE BOSS. There is one other individual who cannot be labeled as easily. If we were forced to so do, we might call him THE PLAYER WHO HAS BROUGHT A GIRL WITH HIM. First, let us categorize the girl. She falls into one of these groups:

a—A victim of conflict in appointments with her boy friend remedying the situation by filling both appointments simultaneously.

b—She is a steady girl friend and knows the boys well enough not to cause any discomfort by her presence.

[19] This is a bit much.

c—She is an attractive hooker.[20]

d—She is a nut.

Regardless of the category in which she belongs, she will spend her evening the same way. She will read magazines and go to the toilet now and then. She cannot turn on TV as this is distracting, nor can she buff her nails. An appearance of deep thought will substitute in the absence of reading material. If she can maintain this attitude for a period of several hours, it will sometimes prompt a player who is temporarily out of the hand to ask, "Would you like a drink, Laureen?" This does not mean that she will not have to get the drink herself, it simply means, academically, is she thirsty and is inflected the same as "Hello old fellow" when greeting a Doberman pinscher after a hard day at the office.[21] She has now become a functionless part of the room's décor and has lost all contact with her escort. A pistol shot off in his ear or the girl walking around nude would be completely ineffective. Even in the instance of her suddenly developing a third leg, this would only create an impression if she walked about on the card table itself. And she would soon be asked to get off.

[20] Whether pro or Olympics material, she figures this is how her client gets his jollies and he's no odder than some of the others.

[21] Although some Doberman pinschers do not work in offices.

chapter two

ATTITUDES AND PARTS

LAWZY, MISS CINDY: YOU LOOKS JESS LIKE YO' PAPPY!

The moving parts of a four-handed gin rummy game
are:

A card table.

Several decks of playing cards.

A score pad.

A pencil.

Four chairs.

To sustain our original contention that the game
has been thought of extemporaneously, these things
should be located with some small difficulty with ap-
propriate expressions accompanying the discovery of
each.[1]

Contrary to belief of the nonplayer, game is not
immediately begun even now. As Douglas Fairbanks[2]

[1] E.G. "Ah, here's a *pencil!*" (Not so much an inflection as might
accompany a discovery of the Dead Sea Scrolls, perhaps, but
some excitement nevertheless.)

[2] (Senior.)

first flexed his foil and pranced about in his mauve leotard, so must the four imminent participants perform.[3] We are now in the hour of Open Countenance . . . or what is to APPEAR as open countenance. For each player is, during the friendly badinage, slyly camouflaged . . . viewing the other players as recum-

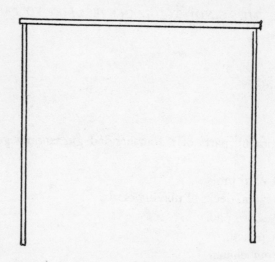

CARD TABLE UNSUITABLE FOR PLAY BE-
CAUSE OF ONE SHORT LEG (SIDE VIEW)

bent putty to be moulded by his surgeonlike manipulations. He plans to throw them a bone of self-deprecation ("I was lucky, gentlemen") at the end of his fabulously successful evening. He sees himself as the

[3] Actually, it is not a performance as much it is a *traditional rite*. As prescribed as The Minuet or circumcision on the Upper Amazon . . . It is the delicious, savoured quality of the voluntary delay.

30

Evil Master of the game. He is The Prince of Hell and almost fears Retribution for his awesome prowess.

This is the Gin God's way of mercy. Four individuals, each firmly convinced he is supreme among the quartet. Mercifully, the gin player's mind is so constructed that as the evening progresses and fortune, it seems, is not smiling upon him, he adapts himself wonderfully.[4] His acceptance of his expectations' reversals are gradual enough to keep him from getting the bends. His progress is clinical. *At the beginning:*

He is going to win all of the money in the game.
After he has dropped a bit behind:

He will be satisfied with winning less.
Still further in trouble, later:

He hopes he will not lose too much.
And, finally, when the scores declare him to be the big loser:

He still has his wife and children, and though now homeless, they still love him.
On reflection, after the first big depths of despair have cleared a bit:

By cutting down on the morning newspapers and cigarettes, he can make it all up in thirty years.

After this mollification, a certain belligerency develops in which his inner voice tells him that he works his can off day and night and that he is entitled to some fun and that it's his money because he earned it and that his wife spends money just as foolishly on hats and that and that and that and that.

The player who *adapts himself* to the growing mis-

[4] This makes plausible the Theory of Evolution.

31

fortunes of the evening is more fortunate than the rock-bound individual who cannot be convinced, no matter how much he is losing, that this is how the evening will end. This is a bitter soul who, on the way home after eighteen hours of losing steadily, castigates the cowards who, had they agreed to play another fifteen minutes, would have suffered considerable losses from his brilliant playing. He plots wild vengeance with the cunning of Royalty in Exile and drives the remaining distance smiling slyly and peering through narrowed, rascally slits that look like ski glasses.

chapter three

SEATING AND THINGS LIKE THAT

SEND A BOY TO CAMP

There is more talk to seating than sitting.

Properly executed, it is a beautiful, final Mozartian chord in form and sound. Theme plays against counter melody and the Juilliard String Quartet is Hellzapoppin' by comparison. The player who habitually wears brown and white shoes begins:

"Where do you fellows want me to sit?"

The fattest member of the group:

"You haven't got a little man hidden in that suit of armor behind me, have you, Charlie?" ("Heh-heh")

The Boss is seated where the best light strikes the table, the ash tray is most available, and the bathroom's path is straightest and truest.

The Constant Loser takes the poorest seat and is grateful to the point where the others feel he is about to lick their hands for allowing him to come back to contribute again.

The Constant Winner is the last to sit. (It is his way of being fair and giving the others an equal chance.)

A moment or two after being seated, someone will ask for a cushion. This question may be delivered in this manner:

"Do you have a cushion, Charlie?"

PLAYER MAKING FAIR ATTEMPT TO
GAIN SYMPATHY

If the Host has been a winner with too much regularity, the same request is made in this manner:

"You cheap bastard, when are you going to get some comfortable chairs?"

This man will refuse the subsequently offered cushion for he views his masochism in a dollars-and-cents light. In some vague way, he feels his penance may bring him Celestial Aid. He bases all this on a wild, wistful assumption that no man would go "gin" on an uncomfortably seated opponent.

To requests or suggestions for better lighting, The

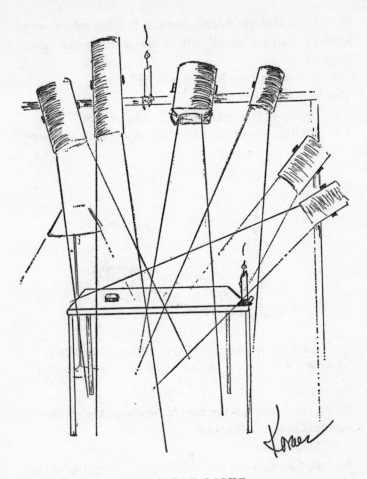

TOO MUCH LIGHT

Host replies with light banter or simply ignores the remarks completely. If, however, The Boss has made the request, within minutes all players find themselves surrounded by extension cords.

The patois of various occupations is quite special and most occupations have an identifying expression

35

peculiar to that enterprise alone. A butcher who is any kind of butcher at all would never let a day pass without:

"You want some bones for soup?"

The hashhouse waitress:

"Adam 'n' Eve onna raft . . . cuppa java."

The nuclear physicist, when an experiment is going

CANDLE HOOKED UP TO POWER GENER-
ATOR IN CASE OF ELECTRIC LIGHT FAILURE

wrong and the plutonium is sending the radiation counters in every direction:

"Son-of-a-bitch!"

And so, too, there is the identifying "Gung Ho" of the gin player:

"You make the blue ones, Larry, and I'll make the red ones."

The opening cry . . . The Yoicks! . . . the first feel of the cards! Playing cards are actually about to enter this world of cushions and extension cords.

One red and one blue deck is used for this reason:

Although the two players using the red deck are at least a couple of feet away from the two players using the blue deck and neither ever touches the other's cards, the two colors are used so that the two decks will not get "mixed up." Hm?

"Make the cards" means "mix the cards" and mixing the cards when the pack has first been opened is a process not less thorough than H-Bomb workers cleansing themselves in the decontamination chamber. Each new deck of cards is packaged in sequence and the intense activity on the part of the dealer in destroying this sequence is exhausting. They are riffled and re-riffled[1] until their edges are jagged and the color is one shade less pronounced. In foreign countries, the cards are not packaged in sequence but this process is not a whit less thorough there either. This is a sly method of undermining some furtive card manufacturer who may be attempting something tricky.

As the packs are being opened, one of the men so doing will say without fail:

"Have you noticed how they been putting the government stamp right on the edge where you're supposed to put your finger . . . how they expect you to open 'em?"

Equally without fail, comes:

"They do that so you have to break the seal and can't re-use it again."[2]

[1] This is a new word. Use it once a day until it becomes familiar to you.

[2] I consider this overzealousness on the part of the United States Government. All in all, it would hardly seem profitable to buy a pack of cards for 75 cents, soak off the stamp, counterfeit

If the statement is made by The Boss or The Constant Winner, the others sit in reflective silence at this earth shattering announcement. If *the fattest person* (and he is *not* The Boss) is responsible for the comment, the accepted rejoinder is:

"Your fingers are too fat . . . when are you gonna go on a diet, Stupid?"

When gin rummy is played with two sets of partners, the procedure is that each man draws one of four cards spread on the table. This determines which two will play together on each team. The simplicity of this rule is rather deceiving. It would be less complex to artificially inseminate an earthworm while wearing a catcher's mitt. Let us see how the immediately foregoing procedure is really carried out. There are four players: Charlie, Larry, Harry, and Joe.

Charlie: "Well, how shall we play? Who is with who?"

Larry: "We'll draw for it."

Harry: "Who's partners, two highs and two lows or the two reds and the two blacks?"

Joe: "Either way's okay with me."

Charlie: "All right, we'll make it the two highs and the two lows."[3]

Charlie then takes one of the decks of cards and with considerable study, manages to find two high cards and two low cards. He then places them face down on the table and moves them about for rather an interminable

---

another deck which would cost about $20 just to re-use the stamp. But I am not one to buck Uncle Sam as I have a family here and fear reprisals.

[3] If you find this section dull, go eat an apple or something.

period. The longer he does this, the more he feels he is impressing the others with his manifest honesty. He shifts the four cards about as though the four men were about to draw to see who was to assassinate the Kaiser.[4] It is interesting, at this time, to point out the correct attitude to be adopted by the other three players while this is going on. All three avoid looking at the cards and small talk is made among them to indicate that they are not concentrating on this simple-minded procedure. It is also somewhat prerequisite to stare into each other's eyes so that none may lose his control through insatiable curiosity and look at the backs of the cards. In about as much time as it takes to hardboil an egg at high altitude, Charlie, perspiring a bit, announces that he is finished. The others now thoughtfully look at the backs of the cards with the air of lab technicians on the verge of a cure for arthritis. Charlie says:

"I'll take mine last."

The others profoundly nod at this. Charlie has said that he will pick last because there is the chance that despite the ten-minute manipulation, the outside possibility exists that he might know where one of the cards may be located. In the light of the fact that the partners paired at this time will be partners only for one game, and then each changes with the other for the remainder of the evening, the long procedure we have just endured seems rather incredible.[5]

[4] That may not strike you as a topical remark, but I feel that things that happened in World War I were funnier than the present situation with which I am too closely associated.
[5] It rather is, in fact.

Now the cards are each drawn . . . some flipped bravely upon the table face up . . . some slid to the holder, face down and shielded from prying eyes . . . Charlie's is left face down, its value known by a brilliant process of elimination too involved for explanation in this book at this time.[6]

Larry has drawn an ace . . . Harry a king, Joe a queen, and Charlie's still undisclosed card can be presumed to be low.

Larry: "I have an ace so Harry and I play you and Joe."

Charlie: "Ace is *low* in the draw, it counts as one."

Larry: "Since when has the ace been low? You some kind of nut?"

Charlie: "Joe?"

Joe:"Ace is low."[7]

Larry: "We'll draw again. I'll mix the cards this time."

The entire procedure is undergone once again and no matter how it comes out, Larry will say:

"See? That proves it."[8]

So now it is resolved that for the first game, Larry and Joe are partners and Harry and Charlie are partners. Less time is necessary to prepare patients for brain surgery. This, then, would seem to begin the game. However—

"Well, Joe and I are playing together. I'll play

[6] Perhaps some other time.

[7] Joe is The Constant Winner referred to earlier. His word is law. Joe's speech is devoid of adjectives. He uses only nouns, pronouns, and verbs.

[8] By now the evening is half over and no one has even dealt yet.

against Charlie and you play against Joe, Harry."

"Not me, I'll play you, pigeon."

And so on and so on. This particular conversation
might be looked upon as being interesting in that each
player has to switch opponents after *each* hand anyway. At least, so it is ordained. But then—

"Larry, what'll we do . . . play the same guy or
switch after each hand?"

"We'll switch."

"That means we gotta keep moving back and forth
all night. Why don't we play the same guy?"

(Joe): "That's okay with me."

"Also, can we look at each other's hands . . . I
mean by that, the partners, can they look at each
other's hands?"

"You can consult but you can't give advice."

"How the hell do you do that?"

"I mean—you can give your partner the score and
like that but you can't tell him which card to
throw."

"How about if your partner should knock and
my partner could lay off a card on one of his runs
but doesn't see it, can I tell him?"

"Yes, but you can't tell him which cards he should
play during the hand."

"I know that, but I meant—"

"I know what you meant, Larry. For instance, if
he has an ace . . . deuce . . . 3, let's say and
you have three 3's . . . and well . . . eh . . . let's
say *Charlie* has . . . well, wait a minute, Charlie
is *my* partner . . . here . . . here's what I mean."

(The others sit like patient idiots through this.)

41

"Let us say I have the Ace of Hearts and 2 of Clubs and 3 of Spades . . . now Joe knocks with, say, six points . . . he lays down the three 3's and some other stuff . . . now, let's say I put down my ace, 2, and 3 and . . . then I say, 'I've got seven points, Joe, so six from seven leaves one' . . . now Charlie, who's my partner . . . (pause) . . . that's right, Charlie, who is my partner, says, 'Wait a minute, Harry, you can put that 3 on Joe's three 3's and that leaves you four points and that means you have less than Joe so you undercut him.' That you can do. That's all right."

"Fine, we'll play that way."

(Joe): "It's okay with me."

THE KNOCK CARD: The card turned face up is the "knock card," the card indicating the number of points (or less) that a player may have in his hand before he knocks. If it is Spades, the score is doubled. This seems rather simple.

"Now, each dealer turns up a knock card, which one is the knock for the game, the lower one of the two, right?"

"Yes."

"If it's Spades, do we take the lower one of the two knock cards and call it a Spade also or do we take the card that *is* the Spade . . . say, for instance . . . say Joe turns up a 3 of Hearts and I turn up the 10 of Spades . . . actually, it wouldn't be that way on the first hand because one partner on opposite sides deals . . . so let's say *Charlie* throws up the 10 of Spades. . . . Is the knock card now the 3 of Spades or the 10 of Spades or the 3 of Hearts?"

"Well, we always play that we take the lower card and make that the Spade . . . in other words—"

"I know what you mean."

(Joe): "It's okay with me."

"All right. Charlie, let's you and I cut and see who deals first. High card deals."

"Before we cut, is ace high or low?"

"It's high. It's low when you cut for *partners* but high when you cut for *deal*."

(Joe): "That's right."

Unfortunately, two players cut at the same time, creating more confusion, but this is finally adjusted Larry has picked the higher card. He is the announcer type and though the card is lying face up in plain view, solemnly says:

"Ten of Clubs is the knock."

On paper, this would seem to take a lot of time while actually, little more than forty-five minutes is used in making this decision.

chapter four

SOME HOT POINTERS ON DIALOGUE AND AN EXCELLENT DEVIL'S FOOD CAKE RECIPE

Play has now begun! Exhultation is in every breast for each sees the others at evening's end in tattered clothing . . . deep dark circles under eyes with pupils distended in shocked disbelief at the holocaust descended upon them.

GINNING, KNOCKING, AND THE COUNT

Procedure: A player knocks,[1] his opponent counts up the points in his hand, the other two players continue until one wins and again the count is taken. Both counts are added together and the resultant total is

[1] The first knock in gin rummy took place in Caesar's time in a public bath house in Rome. Cassius knocked with VIII points but Brutus undercut him with IV. There wasn't time for a second game as they had to go to the Forum to assassinate Caesar.

GIN WAS PLAYED
IN ANCIENT TIMES

written on the score pad. In practice, the process takes on some other dimensions. Let us say that a player has just ginned. At his announcement, play stops and all heads go up. (A scene not too unlike three deer

3

A GOOD KNOCK

and a suddenly snapped twig.) His partner looks at the losing opponent and asks:

"What's the count?"

He must know how many points his partner won so that he will not lose more than this amount to *his*

12

A POOR KNOCK

opponent so that the total score will have a balance then, in his team's favor.[2]

He has, however, erred grievously with the *immediacy* of his question, for:

    a—It is illogical to expect an answer so quickly.

    b—It is psychologically bad to confront the loser with such promptness as he is in no mood, particu-

---

[2] Instead of griping so much about the book getting technical, why don't you just go over it once more and keep your big mouth shut.

larly if he has lost many points, to be heralded on this negative cynosure with *any* degree of alacrity.[3]

c—Furthermore, he has not had sufficient time to recover from his shock.

d—He hasn't as yet performed that thoroughly hopeless routine of checking to see whether his opponent really *has* gin.

e—He still hasn't verified his one sanguine thought that perhaps he may have 11 cards in his hand by mistake . . . or 12 . . . or 13 . . . or perhaps they have been using a pinochle deck or perhaps the other player has a morbid sense of humor and has been kidding or, better still, if he waits long enough before answering, Khrushchev may drop the H-Bomb and his answer will forever remain unrecorded or perhaps those spots on his opponent's face are not from dinner that he really has cholera and the hand won't count or this is just a bad dream and soon he will awaken with his puppy licking his face.[4]

After he has traversed these various avenues, he now has the prerogative of editorial comment on the situation:

"How do you like that, only three cards played and he goes gin."

Or—

[3] In other words, he doesn't like attention being brought quite so quickly to his stupidity. If you looked up those big words, I wouldn't have to spend so damned much time with these @%¢$°!! footnotes.

[4] A poodle.

"He never picked a card."

To himself, thoughts dash about like a Rhode Island Red trapped by a mongoose in a four-foot square unlighted coop. Such as:

("I always knew this rat was a crook.")

("Next time, I'll cut the cards instead of listening to that crap about his kids and his pink station wagon.")

We now have outlined the proper (I) Mental and (II) Oral procedures of the player who is ginned upon. The third (III) is his physical performance. As he *says* or *thinks* these things, he must *slowly shake his head from side to side*.

This would appear to signify that:

a—This is the first time in thirty-odd years that anyone has ever gone gin on him.

b—He has been cursed since he pried open that old pyramid in Egypt.

Tradition has it, that even now, this player must not give answer to the total points in his hand. He is now entitled to a short soliloquy which will *indicate* (only) whether the count is to be high or low. It is not considered *good form*, at this point, to give the actual *total*. If he has *many* points and the count will be heavy, these phrases are quite acceptable and are considered good form:

"I've got a fistful."

"All games are over."[5]

[5] This is used when the points in his hand total approximately 35. The game actually is *not* over, of course. The expression is followed by a sigh. (Not so much the sigh of fatigue at day's end but more the sigh of the thoroughbred who is being shipped to a stud farm in Kentucky.)

"Forget it."[6]

There is a singular absence of sympathy displayed by all concerned at these pronouncements. The opposition only became duly elated and his partner, disgusted. However, this should not discourage their usage. As in all good Greek choral works, they elicit group response from the others:

"Come on with the violin music, what's the count?" If the player, however, has only a *few* points in his hand, *these* expressions are quite popular:

"Nothing you can't win back, partner."[7]

The overture over, the tallying of the hand now begins. The loser begins a slow and deliberate accounting not too dissimilar from the bombed-out London householder gathering his few remaining charred personals into a burlap sack. The player may pause occasionally during this count for addenda to his original comments:

"How *about* that . . . only three points played and he goes gin!"[8]

---

[6] This is a little more serious as its tone of finality indicates. Its brevity, its implication is conveyed with an even inflection . . . a humorless monotone of sound after which the cards are placed face down, preceding the count, and a final cigarette of grace is lighted. This expression is used for a count of 43 points or more.

[7] A word of caution: If a player loses more than two or three hands in succession, it is unwise to use "partner" as the other member of the team would rather not be reminded of his relationship at this time.

[8] This is not really being said as an expression of his own awe —he is reminding his partner, who is growing testy, that he couldn't do much about a hand which terminated in only three plays.

The others, with Lennen sisters-like synchronization:

"Come on, come on—the *count!*"

The soloist:

"Now you mixed me up. I have to start over."

These are *remarks traditionale*[9] that are now forthcoming from the others as soon as the loser's cards have been placed face up on the table. (Face cards count ten points and the other cards as their numbers designate.) If the count is *high* and there is more than one ten-pointer showing, the loser's partner says:

"What were you planning to do, open a picture gallery?"

"Is that your total or your social security number?"

"I've seen smaller numbers on dog tags two years after the start of the draft."

"Thank God you're my partner only every fourth round!"

"Thanks a helluva lot. You been a big help."

If the partner is not in the mood for picturesque comment, he will make a constructive comment and suggest:

"We better switch, *I'll* play Joe next hand."

(Joe): "It's okay with me."

If, on the other hand, the total should be a *low* one, his partner (if he is a kind man or if the two players do not know each other too well) will say:

"That's not too bad, we can get that back."

The other application of this same outlook comes from the loser himself in this form:

"It's nothing you can't get back."

[9] This is French.

If the man who has ginned *upon* the other man is The Constant Winner, he usually utters a self-deprecation which he doles out to the loser like Unguentine for a burnt finger:

"The cards just fell into my hands."[10]

Or The Constant Winner, looking at the other's hand will say:

"Gee, you were all set. I was just going to throw you this deuce and that would've ginned you."[11]

There follows some further play in this first hand on the part of the other two players which is not of too much importance to the purpose of this analyses.

[10] The old form (circa 1932) of this remark is: "They jumped into my hands like trained pigs." This, happily, is no longer in vogue.

[11] The Constant Winner would *never* throw a deuce at this time. He says this usually when the loser's partner has a nasty disposition and the postponement of the inevitable game-ending argument is being held off by all players as long as possible.

chapter five

THE EVENING PROGRESSES—

*NOT GO THAT PART JUNGLE . . . BWANA, SHE-DEVIL,
AND SIMBA!*

There now comes about, dialogue peculiar to the *second hand* of this round which is labeled best, DIALOGUE FOR THE SECOND HAND. It takes place as the cards are being dealt for the second hand. The partners who lost the first hand turn to each other like two members of a Wagnerian chorus who have just extricated themselves from a maze of backstage scenery and we hear this rather lovely aria:

"All right. Let's settle down, partner." (Shoulders are bent forward.)

"They've got false confidence. Now we hit 'em hard and low and keep driving."

"They were lucky that first hand, partner."[1]

---

[1] *That* line will be used between 80 and 103 times during the evening's play. Its delivery will never diminish in ferocity and honest conviction . . . the last reading of it will be as good as the first.

When there is less camaraderie between the partners who have lost the first round, the dialogue comes with a different flavor:

"All right, Charlie, for cripe's sake, watch it this time."

"Maybe you can get your mind off'n the broads and play a little cards this hand, huh?"

"Get off my back and win one. You play like a wrinkled prostate."

Gin players who are in motion pictures are permitted an extracurricular form:

"Producer!? You couldn't produce gas pains with a pound of radishes!"

"You're supposed to be a great actor . . . how about *acting* like a gin player?!"

"Play a little faster. No wonder your last picture took eighteen months."

"If I put your latest album on the hi-fi, you think you might play a little better?"

"Look, the studio is closed for the night, Bridget is back home with her husband eatin' lasagna and playin' with the kids . . . you're only her big boy friend in the picture you're making with her so will you forget her and try to get your mind on the game?"[2]

The *winning team,* at the beginning of this second hand, counterpoints thusly:

"Well, that's a start. Now we march all the way across!"

[2] If Bridget is not Italian, goulash or corned beef and cabbage may be used here.

"All right, Partner, get on the other two games now and we DESTROY 'em."

(Joe): "It's okay with me."

Later on, we will deal with the expressions to be used by the *first* player of a team to gin or knock on an opponent. His conversation is different from the winner of the latter half of that hand. One of those expressions will be put down here *immediately* as it is deserving of special attention. The most used of expressions designed for the situation as we have described it is:

"I got *my* man."

The conjecture of players who are in the entertainment business is that this line became the basis of an early hit of Fanny Brice's. Others contend the reverse and say that it was derived *from* the song and is connotive of humorous lament.[3]

The student of conversational gin rummy has now sufficiently progressed to take up discourse as uttered after the preliminary hand has been played.[4] Therefore, let us examine:

WHAT TO SAY ON HAVING BEEN DEALT—

I (or A)—A GOOD hand
II (or B)—A BAD hand

To avoid confusion, let us consider them in the order

[3] Our researchers were unable to supply definite proof for either contention. We therefore present this interesting sidelight purely for the student's meditation.

[4] A review of the first three chapters is recommended.

named. If the gin player should have a *terribly, terribly* good hand, he may wish to enjoy additional satisfaction. (A kind of "second" pin in the groin of an already mounted butterfly.) He may say:

"I'm thinking of a card."

Can the student here feel the *full impact* of this statement upon the other player? Can he visualize the forming of cold crystals in the bone marrow? . . . the *Bela Lugosity* of the atmosphere? "I AM THINKING OF A CARD" is surely indicative of the hand being 99 per cent complete with all runs already stapled neatly together ready to be laid upon the table. Other phrases to be used with a terribly, terribly good hand:

"I'm really embarrassed to do this to you."
"You won't believe this hand."[5]

"Je suis triste pour vous."[6]

There is a point of confusion which arises here on the comments made for good hands. One school of players make no comment at all and only commit themselves to low moans of dismay. This moan of dismay is ceased abruptly to make the hearer feel that the giver of the moan let it slip out by accident.

[5] It is interesting that this very same phrase is also used when the player has a terribly *bad* hand and wishes to frighten the other player.
[6] This is French and is translated, I believe, *"Where can I change a five-hundred franc note?"*

58

A Good Hand is held quite tightly. A card to be discarded can only be dislodged by forceps designed for recalcitrant birth. The cards are *held* firmly so that none may fall upon the table and begin a discussion that could lead to a call for a misdeal.

HOW TO HOLD A BAD HAND

The Bad Hand is held as sloppily as possible so that a card can accidentally fall out on the table and start a discussion that could lead to a call for a misdeal.

The Good Hand is usually held so rigidly, with the cards so close together, that a hanging Mona Lisa or the player himself cannot see anything but the cards themselves. There is a little byplay here that exists between the two partners in the case of this Good Hand. The owner of the hand will put them together, one atop the other, hand them to his partner while maintaining an expression which is a composite of Hate, Love, Fear, and Joy, shake his head with the tragic countenance of Menelaus, and say in a voice meant ostensibly to be heard only by his partner:

"Look at this."

His partner looks at the hand (which is always already a perfect gin) and says in return:

"Gee, that's rough. Hope you can make a hand out of it."

59

In the earlier days of gin rummy, this little playlet was accompanied by a lascivious wink and the tongue flopping up and down while hanging out of one side of the mouth. This delivery however, has become passé and is only used in some fraternal organizations. The little byplay above is considered quite in *good form*, but any improvement on the histrionics would put the participants in the light of being crooks. (This will be discussed later under "Coffee Housing.") (Normally, that would have been a footnote but the author wasn't quite up to a footnote at the time of this insertion.)

Some more about The Bad Hand. One or two popular expressions by players receiving bad hands:

"This ain't a hand, it's a foot."

"This hand looks like a bunch of keys."

"You gin now and you make one million points."

"Knock now and I'll punch you in the mouth."

There is byplay with The Bad Hand, too. The player folds them together and hands them to his partner, his eyebrows soliciting comment. The partner looks at the cards, refolds them, shakes his head like a Dalmatian with an infected tooth, and says, gleefully:

"He DEALT you this, Charlie? Why don't you knock right away!"

(This is to fool the others into thinking it is a great hand.)

As he returns the cards to the owner, he will portray the holding back of merriment much as Don Ameche in the role of Alexander Graham Bell surprising his wife with a blue Princess phone for her birthday. The fact that a mounted owl would not be taken in by this atrocious performance does not discourage its appearance several times during the evening.

FRESH OR *frisch*

Some players use the compatible system of throwing in freshly dealt hands if both players agree that the hand is ridiculously bad. This is usually determined by one player asking: (It is really not a question but a mumbled comment)

"Like your hand?"

If the other player does *not* like his hand, he will quickly throw it down *face up* before the *other* player can repudiate his comment. If he does not throw it quickly enough, the other player may add "—because *I* like *mine*." It is a happy thing for all when both players throw down their hands. It is *not* a happy thing when after the first player has made the comment "Like your hand?" the other player says:

"LOVE it!"

The interrogator now finds himself on a busy street corner suffering the embarrassment of an unzipped fly. He has betrayed the fact that he has a bad hand and now frantically assumes a grayish smile in a brave attempt to pass off his remark as friendly banter. He will now do all kinds of things to make the other believe the hand he *really* has is worth being laminated and hung in a foyer. The interrogator's *partner* does not go along with this shabby masquerade and gives him what might charitably be called a withering look for having exposed his bad hand. (A kind of look the bachelor gives his pregnant girl friend for fainting in front of friends.)

This little curtain raiser is only that, a curtain raiser. The real acting and choreography of the game comes about as the evening progresses. Let us put the bifocals on the situation arising over the delicate art of considering a card that has just been thrown. This cannot be too successfully done without preliminary training by the study of silent films . . . an analysis of the Japanese theater . . . a course in Zen Buddhism and the running off of a few stag movies just to round out the curriculum.

It is assumed by the gin matriculant that one of two things must be done with a card discarded by one player:

    I—It is to be picked up.

    II—It is not to be picked up.

This is as silly as the assumption that there is only one way to skin a pussycat.[7] The histrionics accompanying the meditation upon the possible selection of a discarded card are as carefully applied as a ballerina's chafing powder. This is no ponderous Polish polka . . . it is, in fact, more Tango than Cha-Cha. To illustrate, we take:

[7] There are *two*.

NORTH has discarded the King of Hearts to *WEST*.[8] Two plays *preceding* this, North discarded a 5 *of Diamonds*. He then picked up the *Deuce of Spades*. To the most isolated of Alaskan Eskimos, it will be obvious that these three cards can have nothing to do with each other whatsoever.

But let us see what happens when Lester West could possibly use that King of Hearts in speculation. Lester West suddenly sees Albert North's discarded King of Hearts. He looks into his own hand and notices, let us say, the King of Spades or perhaps the Jack of Hearts. Dare he boldly speculate on this card? If he picks the King of Hearts, Albert North will not know whether he needs it for a collection of three kings or to complete his Heart run *and* little does Albert North know Lester West can use it *either way!* But wait—damme! He has tarried too long . . . Albert is growing big with suspicion . . . oh to deliberate a mo' or two longer . . . to have a few precious seconds to decide what he shall do! But he mustn't let Albert North know why he is taking this time looking at the King of Hearts. What does Lester West do? He now portrays his greatest role. He will deliberate upon the King of Hearts while delivering running dialogue cleverly phrased to throw Albert North off the scent. He will put the onus of the delay *upon Albert!* As the King of Hearts is a card that has been in this deck and many

[8] The actual players are Albert North and Lester West.

decks before it for years, it is not sufficiently unique so that it, by itself, can provide Lester West time in expressing awe at simply *seeing* the King of Hearts. The very first time, perhaps, that a King of Hearts appeared as a part of the 52 card deck, *then*, perhaps, this might work. But no longer. *Lester West will fabricate a story line to give him time to ponder!* He looks at the King of Hearts . . . cocks his head to the side like a doctor seeing a navel with a left-hand spiral and mutters:

> *"Discarded the 5 of Diamonds . . . then picked up the Deuce of Spades . . .*
> *NOW he throws the King of Hearts . . . hmmmmm"*

Lester West is slyly giving the impression to Albert North that he is confused because Albert is not keeping the King of Hearts with the Deuce of Spades. Now, if Albert is the player of tradition, he will fold his cards to his chest as though shielding them and perform other overt acts of naïve camouflage. If, however, our Albert North is tired . . . if this has taken place once too often in his association with Lester West, he will say in as bored a manner as possible:

> "Cut out the bull . . . if you wanna speculate with the King of Hearts go ahead and speculate but don't try to make out like you're layin' plans to blow up the Kremlin."

There is another unfortunate possibility to this profound maneuver. Sometimes the Lester Wests who do this are not particularly bright or prone to quick decision. Consequently, the time begins to drag a bit and as Lester isn't really capable of weighing the possible uses of the King of Hearts with his other king and the Jack of Hearts while conducting the conversation of subterfuge needed, he puts his mind into neutral as he thinks and simply does variations on his original theme which can be annoying to the other player . . . to wit:

"Picked up the Deuce of Spades . . . PICKED up the Deuce of Spades . . . picked UP the Deuce of Spades . . . picked-picked up, the Deuce of Spades . . . picked-picked up-up the Deuce of Spades . . ." and so forth.[9]

What is the solution then to carrying out this marvelous ruse properly? Simply this: after exhausting the conversation re: the Deuce of Spades, *lay down the hand and while slowly filling a large pipe bowl with a fine grind tobacco, ask Albert North to "look at this picture in my wallet and guess who it is . . . don't say anything right away, think about it a couple of minutes."*[10]

[9] Unless Lester West is Albert North's boss or they are both perhaps, on a small boat out at sea, it is not uncommon for Lester West to look up after all this and see that Albert North has taken his hat and gone home.

[10] It is a good idea to stuff several pictures into your wallet before the players arrive as you may have to do this a few times during the evening. Any old magazine shop will sell you some 5×7's of old racing car drivers, silent movie stars, or obscure automobile parts manufacturers. Each can be labeled on the back and it is an added soupçon of excitement to the evening when you say, after twenty or thirty minutes of your opponent's rapt study of the pictures: "No, you're wrong, Albert. That happens to be, believe it or not, Theobald Prawn who used to make carbureter screws in Milwaukee!"

If the Lester Wests of this situation are not much on remembering dialogue, cards picked, or if they carry no wallets, a simple but effective measure is to lean forward a bit, look at the King of Hearts as though it were a tremendously funny cartoon from a popular magazine, tap it in the face with a bent forefinger, and say "Hmmmmmm" with as much significance as you think Albert North will buy.

ANOTHER INTERESTING HAPPENSTANCE OF DISCARD, THE DISCARDED QUEEN OF CLUBS

Lester West has just picked the Queen of Diamonds and then *discards the Queen of Clubs!* Hey? *Obviously, he is not saving queens.*[11] He very probably has the Jack, Queen, and King of Diamonds in his hand in a run. Why does he throw the other queen so quickly, thus letting his opponent know he does not need another queen? Because he needs the Queen of SPADES for *another run* which he is building in Spades. He is very anxious for Albert North to notice that he has thrown a queen back so that Albert will throw him the Queen of Spades as quickly as possible. So he makes little comments like:

"This ought to show you I'm honest."

"Catch on, Albert North?"

"Guess what I'm doing?"

Also, the manner in which the Queen of Clubs is thrown is important. It is not simply discarded. It is

[11] Or, if he *is*, he is not saving *many*.

thrown to the table with a certain amount of disgust, somewhat in the manner of warm camel dung or a Communist leaflet[12] to give the impression that ALL queens from now on are undesirable.

If Albert North has some brains,[13] he will know that Lester wants the Queen of Hearts or the Queen of Spades or he wouldn't be giving away the Queen of *Clubs* at this time. Eventually, his curiosity will get the better of him and he will throw the Queen of Spades anyway and when Lester West picks it up laughing somewhat insanely, North is obliged to say:

"Nice suck job."

[12] If the game is being played outdoors, one may also spit.
[13] If Albert had *any brains,* he would be home in bed.

chapter six

FISHING, DISCARDING, AND PEEKING

WILL I BE ABLE TO PLAY THE VIOLIN AGAIN, DOCTOR?

FISHING is another free form of the game that is enjoyable. Sometimes in Fishing, instead of the "camel dung drop," the card is discarded with nonchalance, *particularly*, if it is 2, 3, or 5.[1] The motion is a natural one and is done with the right hand. (The left hand picks at a mole or some other skin blemish.) The seasoned *Fishee* (the *discarder* is the Fish*er*) feels his senses reel at the cast! He can almost see the hook sticking through the edge of the card! If he is especially emotional, his thoughts revert to childhood and he sees his boyhood friends again and remembers his mother. And then, shaking nostalgia from his head, his nostrils flare in respone to the challenge! He examines the situation. The 6 of Clubs has been discarded. His opponent is *Fishing!* How does he know? *By the very illogical act of throwing this card!* What does his

[1] More true of Hearts, Diamonds, and Clubs, than Spades. Why, no one knows.

opponent seek? Either one of the other 6's (the 6 of Diamonds, the 6 of Hearts, or the 6 of Spades!). Or, perhaps, he needs a low club for a run and wants to encourage the throwing of the 5 of Clubs, the 7 of Clubs, the 8, 9, 10, or perhaps the Jack or Queen. Possibly, even, the very King of Clubs itself!

Pride in himself overcomes the caution of revealing his knowledge and he may express his contempt for the Fishing expedition by holding one hand over his stomach and emitting a lusty "Ho-Ho-Ho," much in the manner of Santa Claus.

If the *Fishee* is a man of viciousness, he will attempt to frighten the *Fisher* by pretending he is going to pick up the 6 of Clubs and thus go "gin." He never actually touches the card but instead, will look at

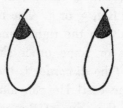

PLAYER "FISHING"

A DIGRESSIVE POINT IN FISHING

it . . . raise his eyes to his opponent (who pretends to be searching for lint), look back at the card, look at his hand, separating two cards as if to insert the 6, smile like Douglas Fairbanks[2] and purse his lips. The

[2] (Junior.)

length of time he is allowed for all this is determined by the *Fisher* who may go along with it all by feigning deep fear that he has committed a most heinous blunder and will, by subtle gesture, try to indicate that he has in reality just thrown away one of *four* 6's from his hand.

If he is an individual of less patience and couthability, he will sigh in disgust and say:

> "Forget the Sarah Bernhardt routine, you know damned well you can't use that card."

The *Fishee* now is afraid to throw any other 6, the 5, 7, 8, 9, 10, Jack, or King of Clubs. This fear will extend to the same numbers in other suits and he will not throw any of those either. This sometimes results in his having as many as 39 cards in his hand when his opponent goes gin and he may lose considerable points because of this.

Almost each of the 52 cards in the deck, when thrown as a Fish, has specific comment allotted to it. Cards from an Ace to a 5 will bring forth from the *Fishee:*

> "Well, WELL. We must be pretty *ready!*"

From the 5 to the 8:

> "Now *what* did he mean by *that?*"

From 9 to 10:

> "Well, we're *running* a little, eh?"[3]

Face cards:

> "You had a lot of guts to hold on to those biggies for so long."

[3] *Running*, as *running in fear*. That is, unloading some of the medium-high scoring points.

A fine technique is involved in this operation. Sometimes, the player ready to knock would like to try for just one more card, as it might make him "gin" and yet, because of his delay for this one more pick, his *opponent* may gin. A wonderful maneuver is this one: Instead of placing his discard face down and declaring his knock, he places it face up on the pile. If his opponent reaches for that card, the would-be knocker casually says "I knock" before the other player gets to pick up the card. The player who was about to pick up the discard knows there is no point in arguing as the other player is terribly occupied in avoiding his gaze and will only express surprise at the accusation that he was trying to see if he could safely discard the card in order to try for one more himself. In earlier times, before this conclusion was reached, the episode went thusly:

"What the hell is this, 'I knock,' you're supposed to put your discard face down when you're going to knock."

The culprit: (looking completely bewildered at this onslaught)

"What are you talking about. I've always done it this way. You never said anything before."

Or if the culprit is a true cheat, he will say:

"Gosh, I'm sorry, Charlie, I was counting my points and didn't notice I discarded face up."

When throwing a card that is positively "safe," it is helpful to establish one's self as being rather stupid. Thus, the card is pondered upon for some time and then timidly put forth as though it were a twenty-dollar bill being dropped in front of a group of fleet-footed urchins loitering in the Casbah. (The portrayal is stopped when the other player says, "What the hell was the dramatics for? Who you kiddin'?")

DISCARDING AN OBVIOUSLY DANGEROUS CARD

This is not simply laid upon the table. It is truculently flung directly into the other player's face with the ejaculation, "Here, you dirty bastard, TAKE IT!" If the other player does not need the card, he simply withers the ejaculator with a blasé glance and takes a fresh card from the deck. If he *does* need it, he picks it up quite calmly and casts a brief aspersion on the intelligence of the other.

DISCARDING A CARD WHICH IS *reasonably* DANGEROUS

When, let us say, Albert North has discarded with some trepidation, a card which looks reasonably dangerous, the other player who *does* need a card *close* to this and who wishes to encourage the throwing of *similar* cards, will say:

"What, What? You nuts or something?"

The fact that Albert North *knows* in his heart of hearts that the other *wants* something like it does not stop him when, somnambulistically, he throws the next "reasonably dangerous" card. *This* one is immediately snatched from the table by the other, who laughs uproariously at his successful deception and then will proceed to call Albert North various names dealing with his state of mental incompetence.

A FUN DISCARD

There is the Fun Discard. This is a discard which COULD be dangerous. It is a favorite of women who dine at Schrafft's. The discarder picks the card from her hand playfully and, giggling as though a little boy were fooling around under the table, slides it UNDER the pile of discards on the table. This is not done surreptitiously, it is done quite broadly which makes it much funnier. Her opponent, if she is to observe tradition, will rise to the scent like Betsy Ross hearing about the addition of Hawaii and Alaska:

"What . . . what was that!"

And, whether she needs the card or not, must participate in the little *pas-de-deux* by at least fingering it threateningly. When she finally confesses that she really doesn't want it, each giggles and opens little white lace fans to cool the heat of her excitement.

Eventually, if one plays enough gin rummy with enough people, he will encounter this type. This is the player who personalizes each discard. The 3 of Diamonds:

"Hmmm. A *very* nice little card."

Others:

"Ah, our Lady of the Diamonds."

"The Card of Death, hm?"

"Old Black Jack, himself."

"Deucey-deucey, eh?"

"AH, ha! The Good King of Spades is no longer in the game."

"Now *that* could be a veerry daangerrous card, me amigo."

"Le quatro . . . le quatro de coeur . . . interesting."

PEEKING THROUGH THE PILE OF DISCARDS

Let *no one* ever convince the student that he is above this. Peeking Through The Discards is *helpful*. It is done in a variety of ways.

EXECUTIVE PEEK

This is the I've-got-every-right-in-the-world-to-do-this approach. A minute and careful pushing about of the cards to see if it is safe to throw a 10 of Hearts. If there are three other 10's out, and the 7, 8, 9, Jack, and Queen of Hearts are in the pile, it is reasonably safe to discard the 10.

PSEUDO-GAG PEEK

The pseudo-gag peek is done by the peeker in a jovial manner. He deliberately spreads the discards in an exaggerated manner ("Who really needs to see THIS many, eh, Charlie?"), feigning uncontrollable hilarity at his playful excursion as though he is just being silly and is doing a clever satire on people who really do this. He is "only looking to see if there is a torn card, heh, heh." (If he is The Boss, the other player lights a kerosene lamp to improve the visibility.)

There are players who profess never to peek. What *they* do is this: When the other player pushes the discards apart for a peek, they say, "Here! Here! What are you doing to those cards," and slowly push them back together, moving the cards about in wide circles. Neither player's eyes leaves the pile of discards during these manipulations. Between their combined activities, they see each and every card that has been played.

76

THE HONORABLE PEEKER

This player never touches the cards. He puts his face as near to them as possible, keenly looking at each projecting tip of number or suit . . . his face at times acquires sufficient proximity to the cards so as to enable him to inhale digits. For an encore, he gets down on his knees and examines the *sides* of the cards.

THE LUNGE

In this, the peeker quickly dashes his hand into the deck, scattering cards as if looking for head lice on his young son. This wily method insures a fairly good all-round peek before he is grabbed by the wrist.

THE IRRITATION PEEK

This is perhaps the lowest form of peeking. In this, the would-be peeker pretends irritation at some random thought or perhaps displeasure with the muu-muu being worn by the other player. "Phugh!" he says, as he strikes the table a rather resounding blow with his open palm, causing several of the discards to scurry across the table thus exposing their fellow cards beneath them. (He is known as the Spanish type, or *El Gusto*. He is at his best with a *light* card table.)

THE DEEP-IN-THOUGHT PEEKER

Meditating, deep in retrospect, he flicks his forefinger out, keeping time with some mysterious tune he is humming within. Inadvertently, he strikes the tip of the top card and replaces it with an apology, exposing two more cards while doing so.

THE BLOWER PEEKER

He is usually a hearty player and players wary of his tactics refrain from saying anything that might be construed as humor as he will laugh explosively, blowing the discards about with his all-round good-humoredness. It is very difficult to not *be* funny with him for anything as unadorned as, "Pass me the cigarettes, Tom," will send him into buffeting gales of laughter. (The greater the pile of discards, the funnier everything gets.)

THE QUASI-HYPOCHONDRIAC PEEKER

This is the chap who early in the evening tells everyone of his many allergies. Thus, he can legitimately sneeze into the pile of discards if anyone even *mentions* "wool" or *anything*. There are case histories of gin players who have deliberately made themselves allergic to every product manufactured by man (also to grass, goldenrod, and rubber plants). One of the major card manufacturing companies reports an increase in the sale of playing cards during the hay-fever season. A player in the East, who simply could not become allergic or fake a passable sneeze, used to play with one foot immersed in a bucket of ice.

chapter seven

SPEED OF PLAY, QUITTING THE GAME & ALIBIS

*PARAKEETS ARE OKAY IN THEIR PLACE, LOUISE,
BUT GIVE ME A LABRADOR RETRIEVER ANY TIME
WHEN THE CHIPS ARE DOWN.*

THE SLOW PLAYER

The slow player is a positive component of every gin group. There are three reasons for his being a slow player:

    1—Caution

    2—Cunning

    3—Stupidity

If he is a slow player because he is playing with someone whose reputation as a great player has frightened him, he will do so because he is afraid to discard *anything* as he is sure the Great Player will pick it up immediately and declare "gin." As a consequence he does not throw anything at all and soon holds 42 cards in his hand. (The Great Player holds the other 10 but as there are no cards to pick from, the game is declared a stalemate.)

If it is because of "cunning," it is more than because

of his being somewhat meditative. Actually, it is another form of caution. He is suspicious of every card. He is the kind of man who has never proceeded beyond shaking hands with girls for he has heard of their becoming *enceinte* on occasion. He eats hardly anything because he read about cholesterol in the *Reader's Digest*. He opens doors with handkerchiefs and avoids the race track because of anthrax. As he fingers each

፠

ONE ANTHRAX GERM

card in his hand, he imagines he sees his opponent's face light up in baleful glee, holding out a peach basket to catch it when discarded. Any card, he is convinced, which is below 10 will enable his opponent to knock, anything *above* 10, to "gin," thus his final total of 42 cards.

The third reason, "stupidity," is a combination of the other two and need not be gone into here.

THE FAST PLAYER

The foot tapper . . . the chain smoker. Before beginning the game, he usually announces that he must pick up his dog from the vet's in 17 minutes or that he is due at dinner "sharp at six" or that he must be home for his adrenalin at seven-fifteen as he has a heart condition. Any of these announcements, he hopes, will speed up the play. He riffles the cards like a humming-bird with a bowel condition. Deals as if shucking ticks. Slaps each card down as for posterity. Declares his intention of not wanting the knock card before the other player has even picked up all ten of his. (He is willing to betray his disinterest just to speed up the game for a fraction of a second.) When two decks of cards are being used, he is constantly readying the other deck with one hand while the game is in play with the other deck. If he is a pipe smoker, he packs four or five pipes at home and has them in his pockets, already lighted. If he is losing, his play accelerates until "friction burns" appear on the table. His discards look like something coming from a short-circuited mim-eograph machine. Finally, he no longer is interested in forming sets of runs of cards, nor does he care about winning. *Speed* is his only concern and instead of adding up the scores, settles for rough estimates. If the other player stops to sneeze, he immediately ac-cuses him of "freezing the ball."

QUITTING TIME

The lady who, while arranging herself on the back seat of a parked car, saying. "No, no you really mustn't,"[1] is to be taken as seriously as the announce-ment of quitting time in a gin rummy game.

[1] Volkswagens are the exception.

The player who announces that "Win or lose, at twelve o'clock on the dot, I quit" does so with two thoughts in mind. The first: If he is winning, then "Like I said, fellows, twelve o'clock. Who owes me what?" If he is losing, he simply keeps playing without comment. There is a *third* plan afoot with this type: If he is *winning* at twelve and consents to play *after* that, the others will be beholden to him and sometime when he is behind and they have scheduled an early end to the game, he will remind them of this occasion. Many players who make this announcement have no intention of leaving whether they are ahead or behind. They just make the announcement to maintain a shred of pride in the picture of their home life.

THE BACHELOR OR BON VIVANT

"Fellows, I gotta positively be outta here by 9:00 A.M. because I'm due at the office at ten." (General laughter from the group as though this were a huge, impossible joke. Whereas this instance has occurred eight out of the last ten times they have played.) More than once, our happy bachelor has been on the phone at 11:00 A.M., making his voice sound as muffled[2] as pos-

---

[2] For some reason known only to them, gin players, never having used a phone on the freeway, invariably muffle their voices

sible, saying, "My car broke down on the free-way. I'll be in as soon as I can get to a phone to call a garage." (This irrationality never bothers his secretary.)

Some players have tried mechanical means of set-ting a time limit. One method is to hang an alarm clock from the chandelier above the card table, set to

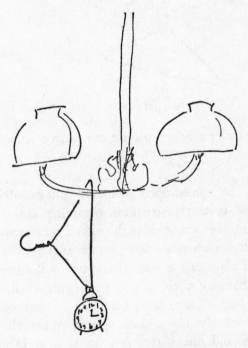

ONE METHOD OF HANGING ALARM CLOCK
FROM CHANDELIER

with handkerchiefs held over the speaker as some conception exists on their part that phones on the freeway precede Alex-ander Graham Bell's birth by some twenty-odd years.

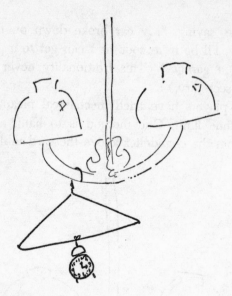

ANOTHER METHOD OF HANGING ALARM
CLOCK FROM CHANDELIER

ring at the agreed-upon moment. Unfortunately, because of certain restrictions regarding obscenity in
literature, we cannot print the actual statements made
by the losers when the bell goes off. It is usually pulled
from its place and is not used again by the household
as the banging about it gets casts some doubts upon
its reliability. There have been cases where only *two*
players use the alarm-clock system. When the alarm
goes off and one player is a great deal behind, he
ignores the sound, defying the winner to acknowledge
it. The winner daren't mention it as this is a very easy
way to get a punch in the mouth.

Another familiar and much-used getaway device is
the prearranged call from secretary or wife. Before

leaving the house or office, he has requested that he be called at, let us say, 11:22 P.M. The phone rings at eleven twenty-two. He glances at his watch. It is eleven twenty-two. He looks at the score as the host is calling him to the phone. He sees he is ahead. This conversation then takes place over the phone:

"Hello. Oh, yes, Miss Finley . . . What? . . . Well, when did he arrive? . . . But I can't possibly—oh, it's urgent? (Deep sigh of resignation) . . . All right, Miss Finley, I'll leave here in ten minutes. Give him my apologies and oh, by the way, don't mention that I'm coming straight from a card game."

There isn't one individual in the game who doesn't know this is nothing more than palpable fraud. His last line, "—don't mention that I'm coming straight from a card game," is only to personalize the relationship between himself and the mysterious "him" and to kind of lay it in the *he is leaving the card game.* The other players will not mention the call as he has made it completely conclusive and he hasn't quite enough "face" to carry through the deception by talking about it to them without the phone hiding half his face. The only hope the others have is to win as much as possible in the next ten minutes, perhaps enough to put him behind in order to make him stay. On some other subsequent evening, at 11:22 P.M. the phone will ring and he will not have to look at the score to see if he is behind for he is aware of a disastrous condition engulfing him. He does not have to look at his watch for he had been dreading the call. He answers the phone:

"Hello . . . Oh, Hi Miss Finley . . . Yes, just killing some time with cards . . . Nothing doing with the answering service, eh? *Nothing* at all, eh? You're just calling to remind me of the Country Club dance next Saturday. Golly, I *had* forgotten. Nice of you to call about it. I'll see you in the office on Monday . . . Good night, Miss Finley."
On his way back to the table:
"Great girl, Miss Finley. Imagine her taking the time on Friday night to call me about an appointment next March."
Actually, he deserves a certain amount of admiration inasmuch as the only thing Miss Finley said was, "It's eleven twenty-two, I'm callin', like you asted me."

THE EXIT OF THE ANGRY MAN

Temperamental players have a custom-designed exit at their finger tips. This is the man who is easily insulted and whether he is the *quiet, hurt* type or the more *effusive blowoff,* his final reaction is always the same. He gets his hat and goes.[3] That is, he is easily insulted if he is *winning.* If he is *losing,* however, he may be insulted willy-nilly and will laugh off the insults and jolly himself along with the others. There is one midway danger here: Any such player has been known, when losing *too* much, to take insult and leave anyway, shouting as he goes, "Just for that, I will not

[3] It appears that I have two or three times mentioned players getting their hats and leaving. This may give the reader some kind of feeling that I am queer for hats. I am not queer for hats.

88

pay you!" So, any kidding around with this type should be carefully considered.

There is a certain sad quality about the man who never announces he must quit at a prescribed time. He never has the optimism to believe he may be ahead at any hour and therefore is afraid to say he will be leaving at the time he is fairly certain he will be behind them.[4] Suddenly, at 1:00 A.M., he sees he is far ahead but he doesn't know quite how to get out of the game. His little mutterings of "I shouldn't have left Mary at home alone tonight. She's nervous what with that situation in East Berlin . . ." I'm double-parked . . ." "I've a long way to drive . . ." and "I must have eaten something at dinner that didn't agree with me . . ." are all patently ignored by the group. The contempt they hold for him is more for his lack of a prepared exit line than because of his desire for departure. Finally when the game is over and he is way behind he *repeats each* of the remarks, prefacing every one with, "I should have—"

ATTITUDES OF THOSE REMAINING AFTER ONE HAS LEFT

The feelings of those that watch the departing one are psychologically interesting. They vary in direction but are alike in depth. They are all deep-rooted. The loser develops a lasting, intense hatred for an early

[4] This is in conflict with what I have said about the general attitude of gin players, but nowhere in the preface of this book have I made any claims to accuracy of content or integrity of content.

leaver as he can cause the game to break up. If the game *does* look like it is breaking up at that point, he will feverishly suggest three-handed . . . then two-handed (or "head-to-head," as it is known). . . . Failing there, he will ask that someone back him at solitaire and promises to phone him the results in the morning.

WINNERS AND LOSERS

There is no such thing as a Good Winner. A Good Winner is so only unto himself. To a Loser, he is thought of only in the vilest of terms. As he is leaving with most of the money, he departs with what he likes to think of as one of his Good Winner's phrases:

"I guess I got lucky tonight."

"Boy, I never saw cards like these tonight."

"They just fell into place."

If he has won a lot even though the stakes were small:

"Gee, you wouldn't think you could win so much at a penny a point, would you?"[5]

If he has won a lot while playing at a higher rate:

"We really shouldn't play for this much."[6]

He also has some stock jobs like:

"Well, you'll get a crack at me next week."[7]

[5] This is to make everyone aware of the fact that even at this small amount per point, his superiority is such that he can still make money.

[6] While he has no intention of returning the money, he also has no intention of ever again playing for the same amount and taking a chance on *losing* it.

[7] No one will see him for months.

"I won exactly one buck less than I lost in another game last night."[8]

These phrases fall on numbed and deafened ears. They have about as much penetration as other stock phrases such as, "Drive carefully, the life you save may be your own" or "Every cloud has a silver lining" . . . and so forth.

A wonderfully curious naïveté is exhibited by The Big Winner. All through the night he has been capable of getting immediate totals simply by looking at a laid down hand. . . . He has corrected the scorekeeper's addition while looking at the pad upside down. . . . He has known accurately just exactly how many points he could be holding in the event that his opponent went gin without losing the entire game. . . . He has been able to work a Double Cross-stix with one hand while playing gin with the other, but now, the game is over. He has won 100 points at five cents a point. Now he takes on the mantle of the bewildered child . . . he wants to look as simple-minded as possible so that he will be invited back again. . . .

> "Let's see . . . one hundred points at five cents a point . . . that's five times zero . . . five times *another* zero and five times one . . . total—oh, I guess that would be five hundred dollars, wouldn't it?"

Another method of taking the sting from the feelings of the loser and at the same time ensuring prompt payment is to say:

[8] This is to erase any resentment over his winning. Actually, there was no game "last night," he was with his brother-in-law, bowling.

"Five hundred dollars. That's three hundred less that you beat me for last week, you rascal."

If the "rascal" has been successfully duped by this, he will write out a check for five hundred dollars, chuckling to himself at his cleverness. If he has any sense at all, he will review his wins and losses and come up with some pretty good four-letter stuff.

Some other end-of-the-game phrases:

"You quittin'? . . . just because you're ahead a little?"[9]

"Boy, if *you* can beat me, *anybody* can beat me."

"You must have stepped in something on the way over here."

Quite frequently, the end of the game . . . the final play . . . is marked with a thorough and full silence. The Winners do not want to disturb this silence as any word could touch off a heated debate which conceivably could end with the Loser walking out in high (and unpaid) dudgeon. The Losers don't speak either . . . somehow they feel that if they can prolong the silence, it will turn into just a bad dream or perhaps the Winners will say, "Ha-Ha, I'll bet you thought we were serious. Now, let's wipe all that out and start fresh!" The *lack* of conversation is more valuable *to the Loser* after a game. It is harder for the Winner to ask for his money in a dead silence. This following situation grows as the silence wears on and even after it is broken. It is as new in approach as if it had never occurred before. The game is over. The

[9] It is permissible to use this at any hour of the night or early morning regardless of how many hours have already been spent in steady play.

92

scores are tabulated. The points have been multiplied by five cents each. The Winners names have been written down with their winning sums beside them. The Losers with their losses beside them. The names are underlined, encircled, bracketed, and other fillers

of awkward silences are performed. Still, no one makes a move. The players stand up and begin putting on coats . . . pushing in shirttails. (No one leaves the immediate vicinity of the table.) The onus of breaking the silence is upon the Loser who, it is hoped, will say, "How do you want the check made out? To you, personally, or to cash?" The most disheartening statement to the Winner comes when the Loser says, "Give me your address, Charlie, I'll have it dropped off tomorrow." This is as never-never land as can ever be.

The money will never appear again in any form excepting its present state as a little row of numbers on a gin rummy pad for that one evening. The Winner, with no real heart in it, gives his address, enunciating carefully to give the polite impression that he thinks it is really going to be used.

As a sidelight, there is one type of individual who is most sought after for card games. He is the one who, in the face of our current hard-dollar existence, reaches into his pocket and miraculously pays with cash which apparently needs no accounting for. It is highly probable that he is living a double-entry system of bookkeeping. Unfortunately, this type usually is on the winning end and is more prone to add to this mysterious source than to subtract.

There is the individual who wears rimless glasses and a vest. His hair is parted dead center and he pays from a check book which is accurately balanced. Somehow, he is always involved in the familiar:

"Let's see—I lost $327 to Saul . . . Burt loses $122 to Barry . . . Steve loses $80 to Harold, Dean wins $20 from Nick. Joe has $321 coming from last week from Dean but that was transferred to the other game where Greg owes David $234. I owe Ed $49 from last night but I haven't collected the $56 from Kurt. . . . So, if we take Dean's $20 and transfer that to Doug, and Joe's $321 to Barry, that means you, Nick, owe, etc., etc."

There are many games, like the afore-mentioned, which never transfer money at all. However, they are played with no less enthusiasm and the I.O.U.'s are carefully collected and saved. They are traded back and forth as the Iroquois transferred beads and blankets. They are saved with the somewhat desperate hope that someday the United States will declare them legal tender.

chapter eight

THE ART OF PHONING THE WIFE

TWO IF BY LAND AND ONE IF BY SEA

"Honey? Hi!—I'm-just-about-leaving . . . Well, just about . . . in a few minutes . . . Hm? . . . Well, let's see, what time is it now?" (Much straining and grunting as he looks at his watch and then, deducting 20 minutes—) "About ten of twelve, I'd say . . . Oh, I figure we'll eat a little something, drink some coffee, and maybe play a good-night round." (There is no food or drink planned.) ". . . You bet . . . I'll drop a couple of the boys off first, honey, that'll take a little extra time." (The "food," the "drink," and the "dropping off" each will allow him another thirty minutes of playing. Also, all the boys bring their own cars and each informs the wife he is dropping the others off.) ". . . Well . . . see . . . honey, actually (heh-heh), I'm a little ahead and it wouldn't be fair for me to quit now, sweetie."

The preceding is the conversation of a man married only a year or two and who is, at the moment, losing his shirt at gin rummy.

THE MAN WHO HAS BEEN MARRIED FOR A LONGER PERIOD OF TIME:

"Edith, I'm going to be a little later than I told you when I left . . . Well, at least I'm calling you, Edith . . . Look, I'll tell you what, I'll be leaving here, exactly—2:00 A.M., right on the dot . . . NO later honey . . . I promise, honey. Honey, look, I *said* I'll be leaving at 2:00 A.M. and if I *say* it I *mean* it . . . That means at—about—say between . . . Two twenty-five and two thirty-two, you should hear the car in the driveway . . ." (In a lower voice) ". . . yes . . . yes . . . uh-huh . . . Two o'clock positively . . . Yes, well you tell me about it in the morning . . . Yes, I know it is but I mean later in the morning. Of course I'm sorry to hear about your mother but the fellows are waiting and—Okay, sweetie . . . good night, dear."

MARRIED FOR TWENTY YEARS:

"Hey Harry, aren't you gonna call your wife?"
"T'a hell with her."

There is the phone call made to the wife *during actual play*. The player has the phone cradled between

98

his chin and his shoulder and is continuing the game as he talks:

"Sweetie? Sam!" (There is a pause here where it becomes obvious that he wishes he had made the call from a vestibule. . . . The attitude of the other players is interesting here. None pays any attention to the conversation and none speaks. Somehow, they wish to give the impression that he is playing cards all by himself and that they are not involved. If he hesitates in making a play because of his phone conversation, his opponent will impatiently gesture with his finger to speed it up.) "Well, I told you we'd be a little late, honey." *"What'd you throw? 3 of Clubs?"* "No, sweetie, I was just asking Harry what he threw. I asked him if he threw the 3 of Clubs. Hm? Yes, he said he did." (Disdainful look from the opponent that the husband has completely missed his wife's sarcasm.) ". . . Is the baby asleep? 'At 2:00 A.M., she should be asleep, huh,' is that what you said, sweetie? That's very good . . . Hah-ha . . ." (Very long pause during which he presses phone tighter against ear to muffle leaking sound) ". . . Of course I care about the baby, dear" . . . *"I knock with four"* . . . "The baby's coughing, sweetheart?" *"The knock is THREE? Damn."* "Did you call the doctor, sweetheart?" *"I do NOT have to show my hand, that's some cockamamie rule you have at your club . . . well—"* "That's a shame, dear" . . . *"well we're not playing at your Goddamned club!"* "He said she had pneumonia. That's a shame, dear." *"Go on, take a card, I am*

99

NOT going to turn up my hand!" "Oh, he said it's a lucky thing she DIDN'T have pneumonia . . . isn't that swell, darling?" "*Stop looking at the discards, is that another one of your club rules!?*" "What time, sweetheart? Oh, I should imagine in about fifty-five or fifty-seven minutes we should be about through. What time we winding up, fellows?" (No one bothers to even look up. He is not expecting an answer and needs the time to think without distraction.) "What Bob? . . . Oh, honey, two of the fellows don't have cars and it looks

SLIPPING PHONE

like I'll have to drop them off . . . If I leave now, they'll have to leave, too, and it would kind of break up the game." (The remarkable thing about this is that none of the men snickers. This, to them, is perfectly normal conversation and quite rational.) ". . . Well, wait a minute, I'll ask Larry . . . Larry, if Charlie takes you home—he lives in your direction? Swell! Honey, Charlie lives in Larry's direction and will take him home so I'll only have to take Joe home! Who, Joe? . . . Why, yes, he still lives out there . . . honey, it's only twenty-five miles . . . well, yes, I guess it IS twenty-five miles BACK, too . . . yes, that does make it a total of fifty miles sweetie." . . . *"What'd you knock with? You went GIN?? How the hell does she expect me to talk on the phone and play cards at the same time . . . you get four points . . ."* (Irritated now) "Honey, I'm taking Joe home and that's all there is to it . . . honey? Honey?" *"I better quit in a couple of hours, I think she's burned up, fellas."*

chapter nine

HOSTS' WIVES

*ELI WHITNEY! ALL YOU THINK ABOUT
ALL DAY LONG IS GIN! HOW ABOUT
GETTING TO WORK ON THAT COTTON!*

One of the detrimental factors of marriage is the wife.
The basic rule of a successful marriage is that the
wife share her husband's interests. How many other-
wise happy marriages hit the skids because the distaff
side refuses to get up on that old steel girder and join
hubby in his lunch hour, swingin' over the Hud-
son? . . . or turning down Dad's invitation for a drag
of "pot?" . . . or her diffidence in accompanying the
boys when they have already gone into the expense of
paying for a motel and some hookers? . . . Gin rummy
is the exception. Here the age old hypothesis becomes
anachronistic. Any wife who insists on joining her husband's gin game faces a future of gumming her oat-
meal. However, she *does* play a small role in this
activity. If she is present at the time of the guests'
arrival (a situation most wives industriously try to
avoid), she adopts an attitude commensurate with her
modus vivendi.[1]

[1] Latin for *La Dolce Vita.*

THE PERFUNCTORY TYPE:

This is the woman who greets his friends with about as much enthusiasm as a *Hausfrau* being informed of her thirteenth pregnancy. She has learned to put into "Hello" both a greeting and a reminder of how late they stayed last time. Most wives do this with the effective grace of a hippo with double hernia. She asks if she can "get you anything" as though she were recorded on tape. The player who thoughtlessly answers he "might go for a cup of coffee" is looked at as criminally insane by the other men. He catches the look and when she asks "cream and sugar?" he answers, "No, thank you, and no coffee either." She doesn't feel the necessity of the usual false insistence of the hostess and as she leaves, says, "Well, good luck to everybody."

As each wife brings out a guilt complex in her husband's gin companions, they are terribly eager to butter her up as much as possible in the 20 seconds of contact that is allotted to them. Consequently, at this remark, the men laugh ensemble, slapping their thighs as though Milton Berle has just finished a 30 minute routine in a high-class night club. . . . They are still wiping the tears from their eyes after the monologist has gone. There is no grimace at the stupid remark even after she is out of sight. It's all a part of the procedure and no hypocrisy shadows their reaction. Only the most uninitiated of players would think of making a wry expression at the humorless remark, let alone, God forbid, fail to laugh at the quick sally of the little lady.

The Perfunctory Type has one magnificent redeeming feature. Once she has left, she never returns. Not that she is fool enough to believe she has made a funny exit, she just wants her meagerly veiled contempt to penetrate further with the final picture of her departing back. (She is the "Intelligent Mother" who, finding her little boy masturbating, does not tell him he will go insane like a little boy in the next town, but simply says, "If you're through being silly, wash your hands and come down to dinner.") This wife never leaves sandwiches or tidbits for the men. If she *did* decide to supply them with food, she would prepare something terribly continental to show them the contrast of her complex accomplishments as opposed to their stupid game.

THE MARTYR:

She habitually is at least two inches shorter than our first type. She wears a patient smile under her nose like a suburban Moslem veil. She looks like an old publicity still of Maria Ouspenskaya and wipes her dry hands continually on her apron in the manner of a maître d'hôtel who is about to be canned. The Martyr is the kind the casting office is desperate for when someone is to be seen in the background of the bank scene at 3:00 A.M. scrubbing the floor. ("Her son has just been sent to the electric chair.") When she says "Good evening" to the men in a low moan, the impression is that she computes *volume* at a dollar a decibel and she is now talking at a peak of about 40 cents. Her effect upon the group is not too unlike a cold hand thrust into Jockey shorts. Each is greeted individually so that all are equally guilty. Her salutary *J'accuse* over, she takes their hats and coats with the obsequiousness of a colored toilet attendant in the men's room of a chapter of the Ku Klux Klan in Alabama. She removes these outer garments with a slow steady pull . . . (the implacability of a tired glacier) . . . removes them to some inner recess near her bedroom (which is "done" in discarded bones and old hats), and paces off the two steps from the coat hangers to her door to let them know she is close enough to them to hear the coats being slid off the hooks whenever they leave. In a steady U-turn, she picks up, without stopping, a tray of fatigued coffee and drowsing ham sandwiches and brings it to them. The tray is the largest she can find as this makes her look smaller and more pitiful and the calculated weight of it bends her knees like a startled cellist whose instrument has just been stolen. She takes the tray to each and every one, tilting her head toward the second-day-instant-coffee if they try to avoid taking it. Over the cups of their instant, they can see the pleading eyes and the bleeding palms quivering from the cold metal of the tray. (The superstitious think of her when awakening on Easter Sunday.) After each morsel has been dutifully swallowed she says good night as though someone has been putting depilatory on her toilet tissue and she has now accepted the future that she will be bald forever. She shuffles to her little room, falling down to one knee once or twice . . . bravely waving away a helping hand and as, from some hidden source in the house, a recording of the Hallelujah Chorus from Handel's "Messiah" softly fades up and out as she closes the door at the end of a particular measure.

ONE OF THE NOTES USED IN
"THE MESSIAH"
(*With Permission of the Publisher*)

Some minutes before midnight she will pad from the room in crumpled, cheap slippers, clutching a torn flannel robe about her, put out the cat, and leave a note for the milkman. At 1:00 A.M., she brings in the cat (she has been standing, waiting for it in the open doorway if it is December) and returns to her room, lowering the heavy stone over the opening.

There is something of a strain upon the game in this house. The next day, she receives half the winnings, coughing too hard to check the count in her husband's presence. When he has *not* been a winner, she slowly turns her head to the wall and stays in bed all day.

THE JUST ONE-OF-THE-BOYS WIFE:

This bag of bubbles is terribly eager to have everyone say a kind word about her and sprays the incoming group with effusive spittle and is not above giving them a little grab in the crotch. (If anyone is wearing rimless glasses, he gets goosed.) Spilling liquor all over the floor, she hastens to pour everyone a stiff four-finger shot of bourbon and shoves crackers and pretzels into their mouths, cutting their gums and lips profusely. By the time they have received her full greeting, they are half pee'd and can hardly see the cards when the game starts. When she says "Good night," she tries so desperately to be gay that her eyes inadvertently fill with tears and she spoils the whole effect.

HOST'S WIFE WHO IS "ONE-OF-THE-BOYS"

THE HOUSE MANAGER OR ONE-EYE-ON-THE-LEDGER TYPE:

As the game is well under way, she comes in to plant upon her husband's ear what is apparently an affectionate buss. However, as her lips hover over his lobe, her one exposed eye is quickly computing the totals on the scoring pad. If he is ahead, she says nothing until she is halfway through the bedroom door, then she turns and says in an afterthought manner, "I don't want to be a spoilsport, sweetheart, but don't forget, you've got to be up at six in the morning."

108

If he is *behind*, she turns at the same spot and says admiringly, "Well, you fellows have a good game. I'm off to my beauty sleep. I don't know how you boys do it but you all manage to stay up all night long and still look great in the morning."

There is, occasionally, a conflict in this situation. Sometimes, she is shacking-up a little with one of the other players and has to conscientiously check his score, too. It poses no problem when both boys are winning or both losing, but when they are at opposite ends, she tosses and turns all night with her indecision.

Thus we see them in the card room. Now let us see them after the men have gone and the husband enters the bedroom. If the man is clever, he undresses *outside* the bedroom and then enters it stark naked. When she awakens he says, "Just got up to go to the bathroom, dear. Sorry didn't mean to wake you? . . . Hm? . . . The game? . . . What—oh, the *gin* game! That broke up hours ago . . . Good night, baby." In her befuddled state, she lets this drift by as she is too tired to challenge the statement. The next morning, after she has had time to formulate some questions, it is too late as *he also* has had time to get some *answers* ready. It ends in a dead heat. We have discussed the Martyr on the morning after. On the night *of*, however, she waits for him to settle stealthily into bed, suckering him into believing she is asleep and, just as he takes that first breath of deep sleep, says in the low voice that has the applause meter hitting less than 2, "I was just lying here, Sam, thinking about us. . . .

Where are we going, Sam, where are we going? . . .
Good night, Sam." (Cough-cough.)

The very first wife we discussed, the Perfunctory
Wife: "Well, Stupid, what did you lose THIS time to
those tramps!"

THE LOWEST-RUNG-OF-THE-LADDER-WIFE:

She is the one who insists on getting in the game.

chapter ten

THE ACE OF SPADES, HOW TO CHEAT A LITTLE AND SHUFFLE

MR. LINCOLN, WHY DON'T WE PLAY A LITTLE CARDS IN THIS BOX WHILE THE PLAY IS GOIN' ON? HERE, SIT OVER HERE, THAT WAY YOU CAN PLAY AND HAVE A GOOD, FULL VIEW OF THE STAGE.

(If the knock card turned up is an Ace, the game must be played for "gin" and no one can "knock." If it is the Ace of *Spades*, the resultant score, of course, is doubled.)

There are thousands upon thousands of gin games being played every day in the world and in these games, because there are only 52 cards, it is obvious that the Ace of Spades has as good a chance of being turned up as any of the other 51; and still, knowing all this, whenever the Ace of Spades is turned up it is met with comment no less than that reserved for the first Martian to visit us with a jammed ray gun. To the player far *behind*, it is looked upon unhappily; to the player *ahead*, it is viewed most enthusiastically.[1]

[1] That about ends the part about the Ace of Spades. In looking over my notes culled from actual play, the obscenities uttered by the losing player would not be accepted by the publisher.

111

Given the *positive* (as opposed to a more-than-likely) opportunity, the average player will *take advantage* of another player—particularly if the first player mentioned is losing. This, in broad terms, is called "cheating." There is out and out cheating and a vague, ephemeral cheating. (Peeking through the discards, which was described earlier, falls under the latter definition.) Show me a player who is so trustworthy that when his opponent offers him the deck to cut he is looking about the room and waves away the privilege without even looking, and I will show you a crook. Two things are going on in his seemingly vacuous mind:

1—His opponent, he sees, is too stupid to stack the cards.

2—If *he* doesn't cut, he will shame his opponent into not cutting *his* shuffle, and *that* is where his little, webbed fingers will do their evil work.

Any old gin player can tell the advantage to be gained by knowing just the *bottom card* of the deck, for in gin rummy the last two cards on the bottom are never played. Therefore, if it is the Queen of Hearts, it is of some comfort to know that there is no point in hopefully holding the King and Jack of Hearts. And it is reasonably safe to *discard* a queen.

There are various methods of determining the card which is on the bottom. (It is also important that it *remains* on the bottom.) First, there is the happy, vague, fumbling shuffler who handles the cards as if he were picking up ping-pong balls with cast iron chopsticks. He shuffles the cards simply by exchanging two stacks of 26 cards from hand to hand, and then puts them back together in the original order as he delivers a brief but witty monologue on the advantages of compact cars, girls who fool around, and peanut butter. In lieu of proffering the cards for the cut, it is common for this individual to point to an *objet d'art* with a pertinent question as to cost or origin. By the time the other player answers: "Eighty dollars . . . Spain, 1822," half the cards are dealt.

SUITABLE METHOD OF RIFFLING CARDS— ALSO EXCELLENT ILLUSTRATION DISPROVING THEORY THAT "HANDS ARE MOST DIFFICULT PART OF BODY TO DRAW."

Then there is the flashy prestidigitator type who whirls the cards about in loops and barrel rolls, only needing a black cape and a tall silk hat to complete the picture. With the flourish of an eighteenth-century gallant handing a pair of dropped scanties to a lady of the court, he proffers the deck to the other for a cut, asking him for a light at the same time. As the courteous idiot reaches for a match, Mandrake begins dealing.

Another method of determining the bottom card is simply to turn over the deck and take a good look at it. While this method is not the most subtle, it is quite effective. Another method is to pass the cards over a reflective object on the table, thus seeing the bottom card's reflection. (An 18×36 mirror removed from a medicine chest is quite good for this . . . although a layer of margarine or butter smeared on the table top will often give sufficient reflection to effect this maneuver. (However, as it becomes necessary to wipe up the butter after each deal so that the cards will not become sticky, this is rather tiring on the dealer.)

Knowing the bottom card has a rather engulfing consequence upon the user of this gambit. At first, he is delighted with this secret knowledge; but as the days go by, aware that the *two* bottom cards are never played, he becomes bugged by the desire to know *both* bottom cards. In order to do this, he must learn more intricate manipulations to learn their identity and to then keep them on the bottom. As his natural course of desire grows, he will want to know the *third* card from the bottom . . . then the *fourth*. . . the *fifth* . . . the *sixth*—until he has the insatiable, possessive longing to know all 52 cards in their order. This often causes migraine headache.

There is one type known as The Banging Riffler. After each riffle of the cards, he bangs them sharply on the edge against the table. He does this to indicate two things:

1—That he is riffling the cards.

2—That he is banging them on the table.

There is the dealer known as an ESP dealer—(Especially Sweaty Palms). He has only to shuffle once and then cannot deal as the cards are stuck together, and as he attempts to deal, he throws three, four, and six cards at once, in little lumps. While this is not particularly open to censure when playing with friends, the dealing of six cards at some other time may bring about an admonishing finger or firm grip on the wrist when playing with strangers. The ESP Player, therefore, rubs his palms on his trousers after each deal and at the end of the evening collects his money, wrings out his pants, and goes home.

chapter eleven

FOOD, MODE OF DRESS, SCORE PADS, AND SCORING

YOU MEAN TO SIT THERE, FRAU SHULTZ, AND TELL

ME A MOUNTED ZIRCON WOULDN'T TURN YOUR

PRETTY HEAD?

There's an old military saying that "A navel travels on its stomach," and so it is with man. Food must be considered in the case of the gin rummy player. The glutton who surrounds himself with cold cuts, pickles, cole slaw, and other edibles, is not a popular player. (Many a gin player has become angry when, after placing what appears to be the 3 of Hearts into his hand, he discovers that it is merely the 2 of Hearts with a piece of salami stuck in the middle.) As more kinds of food are added to the table, it soon becomes a contest of skill simply to *deal*. The cards must be slid on edge between the bowl of potato chips and the can of salted nuts or sailed in a high arc to land in a clean unoccupied place instead of in the chopped chicken liver.

After the host has eaten all he can hold, he makes the famous declaration which will someday be written as an Italian aria, "Fellows, let's stop playing a minute and clear off the table." It is done quickly by willing hands and two fresh decks of cards are put on the table. The condition of the table is of great concern to the gin player, who will wipe up with the sleeve of a $300 cashmere jacket a spot of spilled beer—to prevent one card of a 75-cent deck from becoming damp.

Whether it is superstition or carelessness because of an anxiety to get on to the game, even the most avid of chain-smokers rarely brings enough cigarettes to last throughout the night. Butts are scraped clean and relighted until only a single, solitary strand of tobacco dangles from the filter. The most obnoxious of bores, the biggest cheat, the loudest mouth who should arrive at three in the morning *with a fresh package of cigarettes* is welcomed like a negative rabbit report to an unmarried dean of women at an exclusive school for girls in Westport.

THE SARTORIAL VIEW

To play gin with the proper accoutrement, one may choose freely from a wide range of pastel sport shirts. Little or no jewelry is considered good taste. The cummerbund is acceptable in Latin American countries, but simple trousers will do here. A word of caution in your selection of slacks. The new Italian Cut, for the male equipped with the standard inventory of appendages in the nether regions, is not conducive to comfort, nor are undershorts which are cut to accommodate the Italian pants. If the Italian Cut is *all* you have in your wardrobe, then, *regardless* of the admoni-

118

tion of various health agencies, at least omit the underwear. It is preferred to end the evening scratching a trifle than assuming a deep blue hue from discrepant circulation. (Besides this, there are multitudes of disinfectants readily available, but plasma or replacement parts are hard come by.) There is on record at one of the card clubs in Chicago the case history of a basso profundo, traveling with the road company of *Tristan and Isolde,* who sat down for a twelve-hour stretch of gin rummy wearing Italian pants and was reduced to understudying Kirsten Flagstad as a result of this constriction. Shark-infested waters are safer.

THE SCORE PAD

Game accessories manufacturers hate gin rummy. When mah-jongg was popular, all sorts of refinements were devised. Again, when Monopoly was introduced, they kept coming out with deluxe and super-deluxe sets until a set was designed for the very rich which used real houses and real railroads. Gin is a simple game. Cards, pad, and pencil. Gin players are too involved with the game itself to buy pencils stamped with gold lettering, "This is My Gin Pencil—Sam Bloomgarten." The only wedge the manufacturers could find was the gin pad. Even here, they found themselves somewhat hamstrung, and the first pad they devised consisted of three columns separated by heavy lines with a thin line running down the center of each column, a kind of no-nonsense untility job.

From sheer boredom, they then began putting out

the same pad with this slight addition: one column was marked WE and the other THEY. (As most people play two-handed gin, it is hard to understand why they did not label this ME and YOU.) After awhile, aiming for chic, they simply put WE at the top of the left column and *nothing* at the top of the other, assuming that, by the process of elimination, the scorekeeper would be able to figure out what they had in mind. (The *fussy* scorekeeper wrote THEY in, anyway, with no little irritation, it may be pointed out.) Occasionally they have reached for the big spenders by charging a bit more for a pad which, instead of *three heavy* separating lines, had *three sets* of two *thin* lines close together and the WE/THEY was printed in Olde English.

Bored businessmen sometimes design gin pads in a high state of glee which they give away for Christmas presents. These are pads which slip into an alligator folder. Although the alligator folder is discarded immediately as it takes up too much room when spread out on the card table, all kinds of things are printed on its outside surface:

"All Ye Who Enter here, Abandon Hope!"
"My Hope Chest"

The real square has the following printed:

"Good Luck, Irving!"

The giver of the more abandoned school of expression simply has two words completing a vile expression, printed in gold upon the cover. (In 24 carat, this seems to take on an almost audible sound.) These custom pads have places for deducting one team's score from another, boxes in which to write temporary scores, places to add, running scores, and so forth. So much room is used up in these little refinements that no room is left for the actual tabulations of the game.

This is a foolish gift and is rarely received with appreciation as the *donor* is usually the heavy winner and there is no presentation he can make that does not recall past bitternesses. The *recipient* of the gift figures it is being given him as an attempt (unsuccessful) so salve him or, worse, to rub salt in his wounds.

Occasionally, the personalized score pad is accompanied by personalized decks of cards. These are decks with the name or monogram of the person on the back. Unfortunately, personalized decks come in the more narrow bridge size; and, as the average gin player has a rather large hand, ten cards of this lesser width placed in his hand usually leaves him with the last two fingers completely unoccupied. Unless he carries a purse.

One of the worst mistakes an advertiser can make is to print the name of his product on the backs of cards. The perennial loser, as his opponent says "GIN!" looks up at the back of that hand and the first thing he sees is BUY BLUMBERG'S BLUE BLADES. He will never shave again without being reminded of his losses.

There is another deck of cards which is smuggled into this country now and then. The backs are quite ordinary, but the faces consist of 52 pornographic poses. Gin players call these cards "Disgusting"; and because

Your GIN RUMMY PAD

YOU	HIM	YOU	HIM	YOU	HIM

GOOD LUCK!

WHO'S SORRY NOW!?

◆ PASS   DON'T PASS ◆

THEM THAT HAS, GETS!

HA! HA!

TOTAL POINTS LOST

YOU							
HIM							

TOTAL POINTS WON

YOU							
HIM							

ORDER SLIP FOR ROOM SERVICE

ITEM	AMOUNT	
	RYE	WH.
HAM		
CLUB		
TUNA		
CHICKEN		
SALAMI		
COFFEE	BK	CR	SUG

PLAYERS NICKNAMES

YOU	
HIM	

MOON PHASES

LAST OIL CHANGE

SCORE PAD DESIGNED BY EXECUTIVE AS
GIFT FOR FRIEND

of their disgust go through the cards so frequently in order to express their disgust that the cards soon become frayed and terribly dog-eared. (They are handy for conversational substitutes after they have become fairly well memorized. A player, becoming angry with another, simply has to shout, "TEN OF CLUBS *YOU*" to get his idea across.)

Returning for a moment to score pads: The pads handed out for use aboard the cross-country trains are highly unsatisfactory as they are so covered with pictures of the train and the scenic beauty along the route that the written scores get all mixed up with Yucca trees and waving cowboys. These same trains hand out ball-point pens whose functioning ability is, to say the least, somewhat sporadic. These pens work at every 1/84 of an inch. The resultant numbers look like the dotted lines architects make when they are indicating inner rooms or unseen shelves.

Some players use no commercial score pads at all but simply take a completely blank pad and draw the lines on it themselves and make boxes for the numbers. After the scorekeeper begins losing, he becomes a bit less precise in his layout and the lines separating each score vary from 1/4 inch to 6 full inches in width. (It is interesting to notice, too, how heavy the numbers become as the *losses* become heavy. This is not necessarily due to the pencil point wearing down but to an emotional turbulence within.)

Any man who keeps score is a fool.

The scorekeeper is usually the host. At the end of a game, as he raises his pencil to tally the figures, all

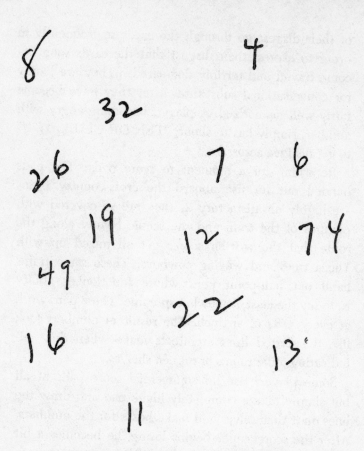

SOME NUMBERS FREQUENTLY USED IN
KEEPING SCORE

players immediately begin throwing totals at him, none
of which are the same. In his anxiety to complete the
score before they can, he adds too quickly and makes
quite a few glaring errors which are instantly pointed
out by the others who throw him another set of incor-
rect figures.

An expression which is heard many times during a gin game and is to be remembered if one wishes to take on the appearance of the pro is:

"You can't add for crap, Harold."

THE VIGILANTE

This is the player who, right after the scorekeeper has added 32 and 10 and has written down 42, rises partly from his seat, twists his head at 180° to look at the score, and asks, "How do you get that?" For the first dozen or so times, the scorekeeper patiently says, "Well, zero and two are two and three and one are four so that's forty-two." The Vigilante resumes his seat, muttering something like, "Since *when?*" After awhile, on asking too many times, the Vigilante sometimes has to go the bathroom, where the light is better, in order to pull the pencil point out of his eye. The scorekeeper hurls epithets at him at this time and the poor deranged man no longer uses words but numbers, and yet it is surprising how well he can express his opinion by shouting, "FORTY-NINE, EIGHTY-SEVEN, TWENTY-TWO!!!!!" The Vigilante, before the pencil has been stuck in his eye, is one of those people who read books like *Tricks with Numbers* and is loaded with little numerical anecdotes like, "That score can't be right. The middle column always had to be twenty points less than the last column which must be one and one half as much as the first column."

According to books on gin rummy, the player should always be aware of the score. At the risk of being momentarily technical, let us show the student why this is so: If the opponent's total reads 110 points (game is 150), the player knows that, if the opponent goes gin, that will give him 135 *plus* whatever he has in his hand, therefore he must have 14 or less (which

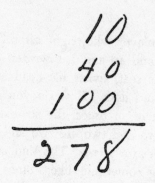

A MISTAKE IN ADDITION

will total 149) in order for the game not to be lost on that hand.

With that in mind, we can understand the situation occurring at the beginning of a hand somewhere in the middle of a game. As he gets his cards, each player leans over the score pad and begins the subtraction and addition process ending with, "That means I gotta have eleven points or less in my hand." In order to have 11 points in his hand, it is obvious that he must keep as many low cards as possible. However, the ones who do the most calculating and make these announcements of having to have 11 or less, immediately begin discarding deuces, treys, and aces as fast as they can get them out of their hands. Someone who takes them seriously is always amazed when they are finally ginned upon to see them counting as many as 45 points as they murmur regretfully, "Couldn't get down fast enough," to their partners.

chapter twelve

THE FALLEN CARD AND
THE WRONG DISCARD

SOMEDAY, PADRE, I'M COMIN' BACK AND AH'M GONNA

BUILD YOU THE BEST DOGGONE CHURCH

YOU EVER DID SEE!

Nobility raises its leonine head when it comes to The Case of The Fallen Card. This occurs when an over-zealous dealer deals the other player a card with something like an excess of alacrity. (The player being dealt to, in the case of one of these dealers, usually

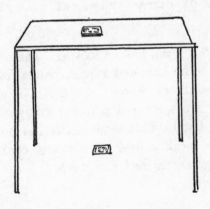

A 6 OF CLUBS DROPPED ON FLOOR

sits like a nervous hockey goalee, trying to stop as many cards as he can, but now and then he misses one and here is one of gin rummy's finer moments!) The card scoots to the floor, where it may be assumed it has fallen face up, just as buttered toast always falls face down. The White Knight arises in the dealer, who quickly turns his head to the side and slightly up,

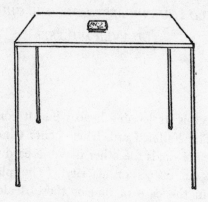

6 OF CLUBS RETURNED TO DECK

saying, "Pick it up, I'm not looking." There is a Lance-lotish lift to his chin and a light coming from his eyes that is beauty to behold. . . . One can almost hear triumphal trumpets and perceive a vague outline of the Holy Grail. (This same dealer has not been un-known to sneak a peek at the next card while the player is retrieving the fallen one.)

NOBLE DEALER WHO HAS THROWN CARD
TO FLOOR AND IS WAITING FOR OTHER
PLAYER TO PICK IT UP

THE WRONG DISCARD

As has been intimated in earlier chapters, no one who cannot successfully play a week in summer stock should attempt to play gin, for histrionic prowess is even more important than being able to tell one suit from another. No better illustration of the need for acting ability can be given than the instance known as The Wrong Discard. Case: Albert North has just thrown the King of Hearts when actually he had meant to throw the 3 of Clubs. He is aware of his error for the first time when he sees the King of Hearts hitting the discard pile. What now transpires pales Gielgud's Hamlet in objective comparison. To further complicate things, Albert North has *just picked* the King of Hearts prior to this turn. Lester West, as the King of Hearts falls, turns his head slowly as if dislodging a hooked neck cartilage and furrows his brow section thoughtfully for this has all the appearances of *le play unique.*[1] Albert, on seeing his king lying there, has a gnawing

[1] Polish for "unique play."

suspicion under growth that he may have done something wrong. He does not look into his hand immediately to check as:

(1) This will betray the fact that he did not mean to throw it, which will indicate that he has two leftover kings in his hand and Lester West will knock now in order to catch him with the redundant 20 points.

(2) Perhaps if he does not look immediately, all this will pass and when he does look, sneaking up on himself as it were, the king will still be in his hand as this is really impossible to have happened.

He draws slowly on his cigarette, contemplating the ash as if it were by Gauguin. As he slowly lowers his cigarette to the tray, he now feels ready to check and see if the King of Hearts he sees lying there is the one he had in his hand a minute ago. A sting of strings and brass!!! It is! He is castrated! (If he is a girl, he is distraught, instead.) The King of Clubs and the King of Spades stand alone in his hand like the two Ritz Brothers when Harry goes to the toilet. Ridiculously, he has a further problem. Basically, he must get rid of the two kings quickly and yet . . . there *is* still the fourth king, the King of Diamonds someplace about. Perhaps, Lester . . . oh, just *perhaps* Lester will throw him the King of Diamonds. What fun it will be to see the disbelief in Lester's eyes when he, Albert, picks up the King of Diamonds after just having thrown away the King of Hearts. Lester, poor fool, will think he has a diamond run! (Lester, actually, happens to have four queens one of which, quite reasonably, must be the

132

Queen of Diamonds and will not be taken in by this.)
On the other hand, suppose, says Albert North, paring
a toenail thoughtfully to throw Lester off the scent,
suppose *Lester* has a high diamond run . . . might he
throw the king off the run just to see what's going on?
Taking a palette and brush, Albert does a fast seascape
to further indicate nonchalance. He feels a bit sorry
for Lester, who is obviously bewildered at his Master
Play. (In reality, Lester is saying to himself, "The
horse's ass, he just threw off one of his three kings.")
But, Lester, too, will carry on with his end of theater
and continue his thoughtful expression. *He* is hoping
that *Albert* is hoping that *he, Lester,* will throw the
King of Diamonds now . . . Lester knows better and
will hold it till Khrushchev takes the wafer for his first
Holy Communion. And so they sit, out-Burt Lancaster-
ing each other. Albert, whistling a slow Strauss waltz,
smiling sagely . . . Lester, Quasimodo while being
whipped wrongly. This boo-boo, incidentally, on the
part of Albert North, is *not* as isolated a circumstance
as its stupidity might have one believe. It happens
with the regularity of *Ramona* in Rhode Island summer stock and the annual presentation by the eighth
grade of *The Landing of the Pilgrims.*[2]

[2] An interesting sidelight on that which we will discuss at
length in a book of another nature. Some historians hold that
Patricia Alden was a little pregnant during Captain John's proposal for John Alden and that the conversation had nothing to
do with a proposal, but rather he was laying out his itinerary
of the past three months, which proved conclusively that he had
been nowhere in the neighborhood at the time incubation was
initiated.

chapter thirteen

HOW TO DECLARE GIN AND THE ART OF "COFFEE HOUSING"

I PRITHEE, MISTRESS NANCY, DO NOT DOUBT MY
APPROVAL OF THE BUNDLING BOARD IN OUR COURT-
SHIP. THIS WOODPECKER SIMPLY FOLLOWED
ME HOME.

The declaration of gin is a personal thing and every player has his own technique. Possibly one of the oldest methods of declaring gin is for the player to put down his cards and say:

"Gin."

Does the student feel a tingling that prickles the hair at that? The flowing juices of the juniper berry were never as pungent with savor. It is maidens, gossamer clad, running through fields of wanton poppies . . . it is the first robin of spring . . . the last train to Yuma. . . .

It is sometimes said with the arched eyebrow. . . . This type accompanies the pronouncement with the flick of a fine lace handkerchief.

There is the more rotund of participants who shouts "GIN!" His is the cry of the Yukon . . . the sighting of the Great White Whale . . . the finding of the Lost City of Krphinniff. . . .

There is, too, the sadly muttered, barely audible "gin" of the loser (who is so far behind that nothing can help) living with the wild thought that perhaps if he does *not* divulge his gin, NO ONE will and the night will go on forever, the game never ending. He parallels

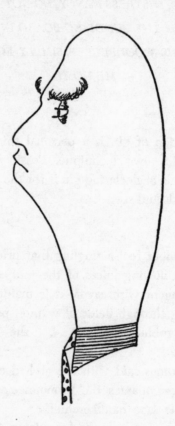

AD EXECUTIVE DEFYING AGENCY MAN
TO DECLARE GIN

the case of the bachelor fearing the rabbit test who is breathing air from the irrational thought that if no one can *find* a rabbit to be tested, his young lady's delicacy will never become a reality. It is what the psychiatrists call, "Lapidum Non Locato, Therefor, Tu Es Not Knocked Up."

There is, shamefully, the *apologetic* "gin" of the agency man to his senior account executive, physically accompanied by preoccupation with tie clasp or pocket lodestone. He is trying for the appearance of inadequacy despite the triumph of his moment. He is the recalcitrant trap shooter who blows his brains out after winning the meet so as to not offend the others. This lamentable type has been known to throw away one of three jacks in order to foul his chances of going gin against the Executive. The next day he will deliberately miss a two-inch putt against the agency's best client. He is to be shunned as are public toilets in the low-rent district of Haiti.

The 1/4-of-a-cent player is in a world of his own. When HE declares "Gin," he spoons it from the Wassail Bowl. It is *troweled* rather than spoken. On occasions when he is pressed for time, he cuts it down to a five minute performance, but he wants all to share in his joy. This is known as Beverly Hills *Gemütlich*. As the evening goes on, he limits his expressiveness to some one-liners of the Moran and Mack, Pick and Pat, Cohen on the Telephone school of humor:

"What's the name of the game? GIN!"
"What time is it?" (The other player dutifully looks at his watch and tells him it is eight o'clock.) "GIN TIME!"

"What did the old lady put in the stew? GIN!"
"What's a three letter word beginning with J? GIN!"
"What goes with vermouth? GIN!"
"I don't know what *you* got, but I got GIN!"
"What's the last half of an innocent girl? VirGIN!"

GIN

He is the player, who when playing partners and has beaten his opponent, says: "Give me a fork, he's done on *this* side."

The methodical player who is a part-time actor holds the moment dear. He has just picked the card that makes him gin. He widens his eyes and rolls them roguishly as though looking up through a sidewalk grating at the underside of a lady from the John Birch Society. He pushes the card into its place with his elbow, slowly as though pouring nitro into the drilled hole of a safe. . . . He clears his throat, hands a blindfold and last cigarette to his opponent, leans across the table like Conrad Veidt in an old movie on TV, lays the cards down with the effort of a fat lady with gas, and says "gin" with the proper hush of push button warfare or the discovery of a cure for the common cold.

Certain older members of fraternal organizations and health clubs declare "gin" with more physical exhibition, executing a series of Immelmanns popular with pilots during World War I and then laying down the cards as if flying on instrument.

Note: It is inviting homicide to lay down a gin hand one card at a time.

COFFEE HOUSING

"Coffee Housing" is "coffee housing" up to a point. After that, it is cheating. It is "coffee housing" to throw a 3 of Clubs, saying with not too accomplished a delivery, "Phew! Who wants 3's!" When the other player throws the 3 of Diamonds, it is then acceptable to grab it, shouting happily, "Ha-Ha, Jack, I only meant who wants 3's of *Clubs!*" (Technically, *this* example is a combination of "coffee housing" and "fishing.") It is no longer considered "coffee housing," however, if the same playlet is performed with the discarder of the 3 reading his line rather *seriously* and omitting the tip-off word, "Phew."

Another example: The coffee houser has thrown his card . . . he gasps, snaps his fingers, and says, quite seriously, "Damn. I blew it. Now I can't go gin." This influences his opponent to relax and throw cards he normally would be more cautious of throwing. Suddenly, one of these cards is snatched up by the "Coffee Houser," who says (every time), "The *only* card that could give me gin. I thought it had already been played." This is known as Advanced Coffee Housing, or "cheating." The perfectionist is rather superb in his various portrayals, his depictions of anguish making *Oedipus Rex* look like Walt Disney cartoons. He can run the gamut from a fleeting, furtive furrow of puckered pain to an all-out Opheliaistic mad scene, humming throughout, the "Bell Song" from *Lakmé*.

"Coffee housing" is used also in reverse. That is, when the "Coffee Houser" has a *poor* hand, he will chuckle like the late Sidney Greenstreet pulling off a fly's legs under an overhead fan, wipe tears of mirth from his eyes, and do everything but order flowers for his unfortunate opponent, to plant the subtle thought that he has a great gin hand.

chapter fourteen

ALOHA[1]

*AND AUNT POLLY SAID SHE KNEW I WAS A BOY
INSTEAD OF A GIRL WHEN SHE THREW ME THE
BALL OF KNITTING AND I CLOSED MY LEGS TO
CATCH IT INSTEAD OF SPREADING THEM APART.
WHAT'D SHE MEAN BY THAT, HUCK?*

LITTLE ADDENDA

Some small bits of information to round out this
treatment and to possibly answer some of your questions.

52 CARDS

The deck should consist of 52 cards. If, upon counting
the cards, it is discovered that there are only 51, the
game may still be played by the *honor system* (or
lese majestic). The *lese majestic* method of playing is
this: Each player takes half the deck (inasmuch as one
card is missing, it will not be possible for *each* to have
26 cards. One must have 25 and the other 26.) Then,
by putting each of the halves in suits and complete
sequences, it will be determined which card is missing. It may come about in this manner:

"Say, Bob, do you have the 8 of Clubs?"

[1] This is "good-by" or a belly laugh (a low ha).

"Yes, I do, Tom."

"Then I guess that isn't the card that's missing, Bob."

"Good thinking, Tom, let's look further."

Finally, it is deduced that the missing card is the 6 of Spades. They begin playing and should Tom or Bob, during the course of the game, have need for the 6 of Spades, he simply imagines that it is in his hand. A great deal of good fun develops when Bob knocks, saying, "And the 6 of Spades goes right there, between the 5 of Spades and the 7."

"Ho, ho, Bob," laughs Tom, "you are wrong, for the 6 of Spades goes with my 6 of Hearts and my 6 of Diamonds, for without it, I would not have *three 6's* as I indeed do have."

Laughing gayly, Tom and Bob begin pummeling one another with various objects which are within easy reach until finally, tired and injured from the robust fun, they avow never to speak to each other again.

If the *lese majestic* solution to a missing card is not desired, it is solved simply by taking a long Rye Crisp and printing the 6 of Spades upon it, drawing the little black figures carefully on spaces where the small holes are not located. Sometimes, when there are no cards at all available, 52 Rye Crisps are drawn upon, after which, most of the time is occupied in shuffling and looking for broken pieces.

53 CARDS

Sometimes, it so happens that on counting the cards, it is discovered that there are 53 cards in the deck. This poses no problem excepting when, after checking all 53 cards, there is no duplication found.

POOR GIN PLAYERS	EXCELLENT GIN PLAYERS
Oswald Jacoby	Ernie Kovacs
Joan Crawford	
Joe Mikalos	
Dean Martin	
Dinah Shore	
Richard Conte	
Mervyn LeRoy	
Tony Curtis	
Frank Sinatra	
Lee J. Cobb	
Tony Martin	
Yves Montand	
Barry Shear	
Matty Fox	
Shirley MacClaine	
Yul Brynner	
William Wyler	
Kurt Frings	
Kim Novak	
Robert Wagner	
Greg Bautzer	
Harold Mirisch	
Milton Berle	
Billy Wilder	
Eddie Fisher	
Sam Goldwyn	
David Selznick	
Richard Quine	
Jack Lemmon	
Minna Wallis	
Alec Guinness	

Beldon Kattleman
Ray Ryan
John Scarne
Edie Adams
Eddie Alperson
Tony Owen
Steve Blauner
Paul Monash
Peter Lawford
Jack Gordean
Julie Styne
David Rose
Sol Schwartz
Abe Schneider
Burt Schneider
Leo Jaffe
Sam Briskin
Sol Siegel
Charlie Feldman
Doctor Chas. Markman
Charlie Lederer
Jaques Leslie
Carolyn Jones
Jimmy Wolf
William Goetz
Doug Whitney
Pat Di Cicco
Maggi Brown
Joe Behar
Sidney Chaplin
Quique Jourdan
Mike Frankovitch